LEMON,
LOVE &
OLIVE OIL

kouprovri

green

of green
ter

o to accept before water
juice of 1 lemon + mix + wat
1/2 spoon salt 1/2 spoon

to...

sks w/ cabbage s
+ lin

disks w/ avo cre
+ pepri
w/ gouda + mustard dlap dip
+ porchetta

scordalia water
oil.

2 potatoes, - cle
w/ salt, bor

mash w/ fork the
add grated
add olive oil gerlic
ake - dates + tahi - add
1 lemon 5 spo
- salt

cabbage
, jalapens -
ers , gouda
3 spoons water
boiling
water 8 ou
cake notes:

Also by Mina Stone
Cooking for Artists

LEMON, LOVE & OLIVE OIL

MINA STONE

HARPER WAVE

An Imprint of HarperCollins*Publishers*

HarperCollins books may be purchased for educational, business, or sales promotional use. For information, please email the Special Markets Department at SPsales@harpercollins.com.

First Harper Wave hardcover published 2021.

FIRST EDITION

Designed by Dominique Clausen

Library of Congress Cataloging-in-Publication Data has been applied for.

ISBN 978-0-06-297326-9

21 22 23 24 25   TC   10 9 8 7 6 5 4 3 2 1

Dedicated to my parents, James and Evgenia Stone

"What sustains me is knowing we exist in duality. It is not just one thing that's happening—clearly so much is happening. Being present to pain and joy, trauma and potential, crisis and purpose, darkness and light, life and death. To tune into what's underneath the surface? what's beyond the five senses? and connect to the depths of the heart."

—Daphne Lopez

CONTENTS

COOKING WITH LOVE

Katerina, my friend Ioanna's mother, was cutting up out-of-season, watery tomatoes from the grocery store down the street. Earlier that evening she had specified clearly, "Pick out the tomatoes that smell like tomatoes, those are the ones I want for our salad!" Ioanna called her from the store to announce that, in fact, none of the tomatoes smelled like tomatoes, but she bought them and brought them home anyway.

I watched my friend's mother quietly cook an elaborate meal in her daughter's small, rickety Brooklyn kitchen, making herself at home in a foreign town by calling on the familiar ritual. The joy and warmth emanating from Katerina was palatable—she was reunited with her daughter, she was witnessing Ioanna's new life in New York City, and she was meeting her friends for the first time. She set the table with lots of wine, bite-size spinach pies, Greek salad, and *pasticcio* (a delightful Greek pasta dish with meat sauce and béchamel) and ushered us to sit and eat.

We laughed throughout dinner, drinking and eating in happy excess.

We marveled at Katerina's ability to transform mediocre, corner-store ingredients into the comforting and familiar deliciousness of a traditional Greek meal. The tomatoes were flavorless, the cucumbers were soft, the feta was dry and spongy— but we tasted something else beyond all that, something that can only be described as love.

The dinner Katerina made for us that night remains vivid in my memory. My theory is that her confidence and serenity in the kitchen and the fact that she was cooking for her daughter, for someone she loved, had magically elevated the meal to utter deliciousness. It tasted like home, like there was time and energy infused right into every bite, even though the ingredients had tried to fight against her.

How I view this cookbook could be most accurately described as a journal. A record of what I have been cooking over the years for my friends and family, and in my work as a chef.

Over time, the recipes start to take shape on the page, and I find that my life, past and present, weaves its way into the pages of the book, traveling seamlessly alongside the food.

I titled my first cookbook *Cooking for Artists*, because that was what I had been doing over the years—cooking for different artists and recording those recipes. It was a title aptly describing that period of time and the freedom I was given to develop my style of cooking: one I describe as simple food with an attention to detail. Its purpose is to be direct, uncomplicated, and soothing.

Throughout these past few years, I have continued cooking for artists and galleries. I partnered in the opening of *Mina's*, a restaurant at PS1 in New York City. I also gathered around the dinner table with my partner, Alex, my step-daughter, Sophia, and my son, Apollo.

Cooking has started to take on a different meaning for me; it's become even more important than I could have imagined. It has become a necessity as well as a source of familiar comfort. A place to connect with my family, friends, and community.

I've seen cooking soothe and strengthen people during times of crisis, and I've seen it serve as a form of activism and dissent. Cooking and eating are, after all, a glue that holds us together in tough times and gives our days hope. It is the place we come back to in order to replenish. It is how we honor the essence of ourselves, and it is how we show love.

This book documents the recipes from different avenues of my life. They weave the web of who I am and continue the traditions of what was taught to me by the generations before me. The most important thing I've learned from the women in my family is to cook with love, abandon, and an absence of fear. It's OK to not have all the right ingredients: you can substitute another one. It's OK to not have the right cooking equipment—my yiayia made the best food, every summer, out of a toaster oven.

The most important thing is understanding that experiencing good food is a sum of its parts and nothing should get in your way. It is the intention you bring to the table that ultimately makes the difference between an average meal and a memorable one.

INTRODUCTION

by James Stone

Mina asked me to write an introduction to *Lemon, Love & Olive Oil*, her second cookbook. I am both flattered and a little overwhelmed by this task. I am not a chef; I am not a food writer. I know very little about the culinary arts except what I've learned, here and there, by watching Mina cook and dance at the same time. In the kitchen her limbs flail, intertwining, at times indistinguishable. She communicates with a wink and a nod, waving a hot pan in one hand, holding a chunk of fish in the other.

You cannot curb this young woman's enthusiasm, or love, for what she does. In this book, it bubbles over into the recipes.

Followers of my daughter's creations over the years may be interested to know a little about the evolution of Mina's career. As I was leafing through old manila folders from her elementary school days, I came across this fragile document:

MID-YEAR REPORT
Student: Mina Stone

Mina was twelve years old at the time. Apart from its amusement value, the yellowed school report revealed much about the history of who she has become and the engaging, radiant, good-humored character she brings to *Lemon, Love & Olive Oil*.

While Mina has been quite successful in her science experiences this year, at times she allows silliness to keep her from succeeding. Examples of this include several instances of disruptive, uncontrolled giggling . . .

The powerful thinking represented in her literature homework has been of the highest caliber; however, she needs to pay more attention to proofreading and overall neatness on these assignments.

The most memorable moment of Mina's work in vocabulary came during the SSAT. There was an analogy that read: "sugar is to vinegar as . . ." There were a variety of choices. She called over the teacher for assistance. The teacher, who was unable to offer any real help, said, "Relax, it's just an analogy . . . you've done those before . . ." Mina sighed and said, "Yeah, but how am I supposed to know if these test people think vinegar is sweet or sour?" As usual, Mina had a good point to make!

Throughout this book I see markers of who I've always known my daughter to be. Creative, serious, compassionate, thoughtful, and without fail humorous and fostering connection.

For Mina everything is about relationships. From the initial spark of connecting with the other to the sharing of thoughts, personal anecdotes, recipes, and preparing and serving food—everything designed and enacted for the sole purpose of pleasing people and bringing them together to enjoy food, share stories, lean in, and listen closely to one another. To feel warm and content.

—James Stone, psychologist, poet, and Mina's dad

LEMON, LOVE & OLIVE OIL

with illustrations by
URS FISCHER

and photography by
CASSANDRA MacLEOD

GROCERY SHOPPING

Bodega: a small grocery store in an urban area, a convenience store

Sophia FaceTimes me. Her bangs look wet and she's wearing plaid pants.
"What's on your bangs?"
"Grease."
"Grease?"
"Grease," she says again.
She's thirteen. Remember thirteen? The worst and the best age.

In my mind she's eating Takis Fuego. She likes to go to the bodega with Ariel and get turkey on a roll with lettuce. Nothing else, but she puts Takis on the sandwich as a condiment. They go up to her room while I call after them, wondering, what music they are listening to now? Wanting in on that teen responsibility of just existing. They politely ignore me, and I hear them unwrapping their sandwiches.

When you live in New York City, you often shop at a bodega, the convenience store on the corner that's closest to your apartment. Most, if not all, of the neighborhood shops there for *something* throughout the week. Often the bodega owner knows you by name and nods knowingly at your regular purchases—a gesture that is both comforting and invasive.

When I moved to New York City, the bodegas always reminded me of Greek *periptera*, which are little kiosks that sell snacks, drinks, and newspapers. They have the same cultural function, a place to walk to in the neighborhood, to pick up something small, something you need, or something you forgot.

The produce you find at a bodega is not particularly spectacular, but it can often serve its purpose just well enough for the task at hand. Going to the bodega is also an opportunity to visit with neighbors, a sure place to run into one or two people who live on your street, and a place all teenagers seem to flock to.

I love my local bodega—their wilty cilantro is often just what I need to complete my dinner quest—and above all, the quick visit means I get to weave a little New York City into my day. That brief exchange between myself, my neighbors, and the owner of the bodega reminds me that cooking and shopping for food are an infinite combination of small experiences that go beyond good and bad— it is a balancing act, a trade, a better understanding of the world.

MY KITCHEN

I've always found pantry lists in cookbooks to be intimidating. As a self-trained home cook, I never sought out hard-to-find ingredients—it never crossed my mind as an option. The ingredients in my recipes and the food found in my pantry reflect my surroundings—touched with a dose of Greekness. (It can't be helped.)

Here are some thoughts on how I approach cooking in my kitchen, what I like to keep in my cupboards, what I run out to the store for, and some clarification on how I wrote the recipes.

Ingredients in my recipes are often interchangeable and malleable. I think it is important to keep that ethos alive in the kitchen so one can start to feel comfortable using a recipe as a guide rather than a rule book.

Sea Salt and Kosher Salt

Sea salt is more salty and kosher salt is less salty.

Because kosher salt is less salty it gives you more control over the seasoning. For example, it is great for seasoning meat because you can use more and achieve a lovely salt crust as well as the right amount of seasoning without oversalting. It is the salt I end up using the most.

In the recipes of this book, I most often only specify salt because I think you should have the flexibility to use what you have on hand, armed with the right information. When using kosher salt, you will use more than sea salt or table salt. At times, when I am making soup, I find this tiring because it actually takes a lot of kosher salt to season the soup to my liking. Sea salt brings you there quicker.

When I think the difference in salinity is important, I specify in the recipe which kind to use.

Extra Virgin Olive Oil, Preferably Greek

Olive oil is my main squeeze, and I love it in everything from savory to sweet. Good Greek olive oil tastes like heavy cream and has a clean finish. It smells even and clear—without the rancid undertones that are common in blended and old olive oils. High-quality, cold-pressed extra virgin olive oil will make a huge difference in the taste of your cooking and change it for the better—with little effort.

I like to use olive oil sparingly during cooking (this makes the dish lighter) and add the bulk of it at the end, once cooking is completed. I use much more olive oil in the recipes than people are accustomed to using. I suggest adding more than you would think when you're cooking from this book.

Middle Eastern and Greek grocery stores are a great place to buy olive oil; they typically have large tins of high-quality oil at a good price. If you are at your local grocery store, try to find extra virgin olive oil that is from one particular region (not a blend).

Lemons

I use lemons to season almost everything—and that is apparent in this book. They are used in almost every single recipe.

Salads, meat, fish, soups, pastas, and vegetables—lemons are intrinsic to a vibrant, tangy, and alive flavor. They add floral buoyancy but above all a fresh form of acid that I usually prefer to vinegar. When using lemons for zest, I try to always use organic ones. That way, you leave the pesticides out of your dish. In the recipes you will see that I have most often written "juice of 1 lemon, or juice of 2 lemons." That roughly translates like this: 1 lemon = 2 tablespoons fresh juice and 2 lemons = ¼ cup fresh juice. The measurement doesn't need to be exact; the recipe should be used as a guideline, with your tastebuds ultimately determining how much to use.

Butter

I use salted and unsalted butter interchangeably. I adjust accordingly, using a little more or a little less salt depending on which butter I use.

In the recipes that include butter, you will notice I do not specify which kind to use—use what you have in your refrigerator, what you prefer, or what you usually buy. European butters have a higher butterfat content and are richer in flavor. Regular butter is also delicious and versatile.

Canned Tomatoes

Having canned tomatoes on hand makes it easy to bring a meal together quickly. So much of the food I like to cook is tomato-based—simple and saucy. A few ingredients can be easily married together with this pantry item to create a main meal. I use three kinds the most: whole peeled tomatoes, chopped tomatoes, and pureed tomatoes. I am specific in my recipes about which to use; however, when I cook, I use them interchangeably if I don't have the "right" one.

Feta

People ask me a lot of questions about feta—most often about which kind to buy. The difference between good-quality feta and mediocre feta is immense. Good-quality feta has the characteristic tang, but it is smooth and creamy—not dry or acidic. I like to find feta that is a combination of sheep's and goat's milk (traditionally Greek) or just made of goat's milk. If you are lucky enough to live near a Greek or Middle Eastern grocery store that has a variety of feta available, look for my favorite, Arahova feta, which is sharp but creamy and a pristine example of excellent feta cheese. Dodoni is a good, basic Greek brand that is of much higher caliber than the feta you'll find at the grocery store. I tend to avoid feta made with just cow's milk.

SPICES AND HERBS

Green Herbs: Parsley, Mint, Cilantro, and Basil

I try to have one fresh green herb on hand at all times. It's an easy garnish and a perfect addition to any salad for an herbaceous kick. If I have more than one green herb available, I often throw them all into a salad or pasta dish, or include them in a sabzi-style meze platter. I like fresh herbs in abundance and can often find a place to incorporate them with relative ease. In the recipes, herbs are usually measured by the handful: 1 handful equals about ¼ cup. It doesn't need to be exact, but that is a good place to start if you need it.

Dried Oregano

Oregano is my number one dried herb. Greek oregano has a pronounced savory and earthy flavor to it, and it is my preference to use in more traditional Greek dishes. Better-quality dried oregano, which is milder in flavor, is great to use as a general seasoning for salad, fish, and meats.

Spices

The ones I cannot live without are bay leaves, black pepper, cinnamon, cloves, cumin, and red chile flakes. I use them often and in many things that I cook. They are the spices I have out all the time, buy frequently, and precariously balance on the top of my oven.

NUTS AND SEEDS

Fresh nuts and seeds, like good olive oil, make a big difference in adding great flavor. I buy nuts and seeds raw and always toast them myself for every recipe. I use them liberally and can't imagine cooking without them. They add the element of a savory, salty crunch to everything from a simple salad to dessert.

Toasting nuts yourself doesn't take long, and it is very worth the result. I have different techniques based on the size of the seed or nut and what I am using it for. The nuts and seeds I use most often are almonds, hazelnuts, pecans, pine nuts, pistachios, walnuts, pumpkin seeds, and sesame seeds. I rarely, if ever, toast pistachios. I love their bright green color, and that gets lost when you toast them. I also prefer their flavor when raw.

Here are my general guidelines for toasting different kinds of nuts and seeds:

Almonds, hazelnuts, and pecans: I like to toast these nuts in the oven. They are bigger and toast in the oven in a nice uniform way that is hard to achieve in a pan. I use a lower temperature—325°F (170°C). Depending on the dish I'm using them in, sometimes I'll drizzle the nuts with olive oil and sprinkle with salt, or I'll toast them "naked" for 10 to 15 minutes, until fragrant and light golden brown.

Walnuts: toast walnuts lightly drizzled with olive oil and salt in a 350°F (180°C) oven for 12 to 15 minutes until golden brown and fragrant.

Pine nuts: toast in a pan with a little olive oil and salt over very low heat (be patient; it takes a while) until they are light golden brown, 4 to 6 minutes. Shake the pan often while the nuts are toasting.

Pumpkin seeds: toast in a pan with a little olive oil and salt over medium-low heat, for 5 minutes, or until golden brown in spots. The oil makes the salt stick to the seeds and they pop and blister a bit. If I need to toast a larger batch, I place them on a baking sheet in a 350°F (180°C) oven with a drizzle of olive oil and salt for about 6 minutes.

Sesame seeds: toast in a dry pan over medium-low heat for 5 to 6 minutes, shaking and flipping often, until they are light golden brown.

MINA'S @ MoMA PS1

A Greek American friend and I were having coffee at the Academy Diner in Fort Greene, Brooklyn, one day. We laughed in disbelief as we talked about how the Greek instant coffee drink, the frappe, was now gracing the menu pages at the café of one of America's largest contemporary art institutions, MoMA PS1.

Alex and I opened the doors to our very first restaurant in November 2019. We named it *Mina's* so it would feel like an extension of my home—like the tavernas in Greece that serve a few hot dishes each day. Nestled in the courtyard of PS1— a museum renowned for its experimental and thought-provoking art—we figured the café should embody the opposite qualities: rustic, familiar, comforting.

Alex and I planned to offer straightforward food from the heart. The menu was made up of simple, seasonal dishes inspired by Greece and New York City. I cherished the idea of offering our customers and museum patrons home-cooked meals that reflected the story of our identities and cultures. We were inspired by the idea of giving museumgoers a space to process the art they'd viewed, clear their heads, and have a conversation over a nourishing meal.

In March 2020, the unthinkable happened. After being open for just five months, we hurriedly shut our doors and sequestered ourselves in our homes in order to stop the spread of the coronavirus. Like many New York City restaurants, we didn't know if we were going to make it through to see our doors open once again.

Yet, to quote Jerry Seinfeld, "Real, live, inspiring human energy exists when we coagulate together in crazy places like New York City."

After months of brainstorming and deliberation, the museum, the café staff, our accountants, and our friends rallied to find solutions and help us through one of the most challenging times in modern history. We saw our doors open again—a little different, a little more cautious, like a baby taking its first steps after a bad fall, but we did it. And most important, we did it and continue to do it together.

Looking back on that Academy Diner coffee with my friend, I realize our joyful yet nervous laughter was actually a sense of pride. A reflection of our identity was out there for the world to see, in a place that also felt representative of who we are. The frappe is on the menu where? At PS1? How amazing.

I'll never forget the look of an entire Greek family, tourists visiting the museum from Athens, totally shocked to see the menu—especially that frappe. They hugged and congratulated us—and they were complete strangers.

Throughout this book, I've woven in stories and recipes from *Mina's*. The café is our home away from home and a continuous labor of love at PS1. It is a space offering simple food, yes, but with a belief in big spirit and the resiliency and tenacity that exists in all of us.

MEZE

Meze

An appetizer in Greek or Middle Eastern cuisine often served with an aperitif.

It is summertime, we are in Greece, on our not-so-little island of Paros or our teeny-tiny island of Aegina, depending on whose lineage you're vacationing with that summer. We sit down and order a drink. It's around 7 p.m., which in Greece is the equivalent to an American 5 p.m. The sun is barely starting to set, we are still salty from a day at the beach, and it is time for an *ouzaki* (the affectionate, diminutive word for "ouzo") as my aunt used to say to my mother.

When I was a child, I would watch my mom and my theia order an ouzo and slowly pour the clear liquid over a glass of ice while talking heatedly about politics. (While I, in the throes of tweenhood, grappled with desperate boredom.) Then they would add a splash of water to the glass of ouzo, which would make the drink richly cloudy, a transformation I always found to be hypnotic.

When you sit down for an afternoon ouzo or other drink in Greece, most cafés roll out some sort of complimentary meze plate. Plump olives, cubes of ham and cheese, and vinegary carrots and cucumbers are common, along with the most traditional bar snack of all—a bowl of mixed nuts.

Then there is proper meze to keep one from becoming too tipsy. Grilled octopus, sliced tomatoes doused with olive oil and oregano, thick slices of kasseri cheese, crispy chickpea fritters, or tiny minty meatballs with lemon and the never-ending assortment of dips. Garlicky tzatziki, *taramosalata* (lemony egg roe dip), *tirokafteri* (spicy feta dip), fava (yellow split peas with lemon), and *melitzanosalata* (eggplant dip) could all grace your table if you so desire.

I love this ritual that boils down to a drink and a snack. Often, one thing leads to another and suddenly meze has turned into dinner and you've been eating for six hours, never too full and never too drunk.

When we were designing the menu for the café at PS1, we knew that meze had to be included as a menu item. It signifies a relaxing communion during the in-between times of the day. Not only is it a snack, but a stand-in for a lunch or a light dinner. Some of these mezes are very traditionally Greek, some are from the café menu, and some are my adaptation of dishes from other Middle Eastern countries whose cuisines I revere.

They can be served as appetizers or full meals in and of themselves—with or without ouzo.

SABZI KHORDAN
(PERSIAN HERB AND FETA PLATTER)

In my mind, Persian cuisine is beauty rendered into the physical mani-festation of food. The sweet and sour flavor palette, heavy with herbs and aromatics, is something I have always admired and tried to emulate.

Sabzi khordan is a platter of herbs, feta, radishes, and walnuts served along-side the main meal in Iran. It is typically accompanied by the freshest flatbread you can find, and it is passed around the table. The addition of dried oregano to the feta is my decidedly Greek touch and I often serve it as a starter and leave it out for the duration of the meal in true Persian fashion. Feel free to substitute or add any fresh herbs you prefer.

Serves 4 to 6

½ pound (450 g) good-quality feta, broken into pieces
Dried oregano
Extra virgin olive oil
1 cup (90 g) walnuts toasted in olive oil and salt (see page 9)
1 bunch radishes, cleaned and cut into halves or quarters
4 Persian cucumbers, cut on the diagonal
1 bunch scallions, trimmed and cut into thin batons
1 bunch flat-leaf parsley
1 bunch mint
1 bunch tarragon
1 bunch cilantro
Salt
Fresh bread or flatbread for serving

Place the feta in a small bowl and drizzle with ample olive oil and a sprinkle of dried oregano. Place the walnuts toasted with olive oil and salt in another little bowl and place in the center of a platter.

Arrange the radishes, cucumbers, and scallions in separate piles around the bowl of walnuts. Sprinkle the radishes and cucumbers with a little salt.

Cut off the majority of the stems from the herbs. Nestle fluffy piles of herbs between and around the vegetables and walnuts. Pile the bread on the plat-ter or in a separate bowl alongside the bowl of feta. To serve, take a piece of bread and tuck in some feta, vegetables, walnuts, and herbs, making a little delicious sandwich to devour.

ROASTED HALLOUMI WITH TOMATOES AND OREGANO

This dish is almost as good before you cook it as it is after. But when Halloumi and tomatoes get a blast of high heat in the oven, everything transforms for the better: the cheese becomes crisp and the tomatoes turn soft and sweet, while the olive oil and oregano contribute herbaceous notes. Add some sesame-crusted bread for dipping and you have heaven in an appetizer.

Serves 2 to 4

1 pint (300 g) cherry tomatoes
1 (8-ounce / 250-g) block Halloumi, cut into 8 pieces
Fresh oregano leaves from 2 or 3 sprigs
Extra virgin olive oil
Salt and freshly ground black pepper
Fresh bread for dipping

Preheat the oven to 450°F (230°C).

Place the tomatoes in a small or medium cast-iron skillet. Tuck the pieces of Halloumi and oregano leaves in and around the tomatoes so they all fit together snugly. Drizzle with olive oil and sprinkle with salt and freshly ground black pepper. Roast in the oven until the cheese is golden brown on top, about 15 to 20 minutes.

Serve with fresh bread for dipping.

FRIED HALLOUMI WITH LEMON SLICES, OLIVE OIL, AND CHILE FLAKES

Halloumi is a treat. It is a cheese that acts in cheese-defying ways. You can grill it or fry it and it doesn't fall apart—it just gets a crispy delicious crust while staying yieldingly soft on the inside. It is truly a gift, and an easy one to prepare that impresses people.

In Cyprus this is traditionally served as a meze or with fried eggs and *lountzu* (Cypriot smoked ham). I like to serve it as a starter or a side, with thinly sliced lemons tucked underneath that I eat along with the crispy pieces of Halloumi.

Serves 4 to 6

1 lemon, cut into thin rounds, seeds removed
Extra virgin olive oil
1 (8-ounce / 250-g) block Halloumi, preferably from Cyprus
Red chile flakes
Fresh parsley or mint leaves to garnish (optional)

Arrange the lemon slices on a large plate in a single layer, saving a few slices to garnish.

Heat a large skillet over medium-high heat. Pour enough olive oil into the pan to coat the bottom. Cut the Halloumi into ¼-inch-thick slices and place into the skillet. Sear until crispy and browned on the bottom, about one minute, then flip and sear the other side for another minute or so. Remove the Halloumi from the skillet and arrange it on top of the lemon slices.

Repeat with any remaining pieces of Halloumi.

Sprinkle with red chile flakes and drizzle with olive oil. Finish with a few more lemon slices and parsley or mint leaves if using.

MUHAMMARA-INSPIRED RED PEPPER AND WALNUT DIP

Muhammara is a traditional Syrian recipe that utilizes the best of what the region has to offer, transforming Aleppo pepper, pomegranate molasses, and walnuts into a savory and rich meze. I am drawn to it because it reminds me of Greek cuisine, which has much more in common with Middle Eastern food than that of its European neighbors. This dish is rich from the healthy omega-3 fats of the roasted walnuts, sweet from the bell pepper, and tangy from the acid of the lemon. I adapted this recipe to my palate and simplified it to create a rich and flavorful bright red spread.

I serve this as a dip with vegetables or as a topping for roasted fish. At the café, we spread it thickly on sourdough toast and top it with a soft-boiled egg, seasonal greens, and toasted sesame seeds.

Serves 4 to 6 (makes about 1½ cups)

2 medium / large red bell peppers
½ cup (120 ml) extra virgin olive oil, plus more
   for drizzling on the peppers
1 cup (90 g) (or more) walnuts toasted
   with olive oil and salt (see page 9)
1 small garlic clove, peeled
Juice of 2 lemons
2 tablespoons ground cumin
Salt and freshly ground black pepper
Red chile flakes or Aleppo pepper to garnish

Preheat the oven to 400°F (200°C).

Place the bell peppers on a baking sheet, drizzle with olive oil, and sprinkle with salt. Roast until the peppers are very soft and blackened, about 30 minutes.

Take the stems and seeds out from the bell peppers and cut the peppers into a few large pieces. In a food processor fitted with the metal blade, combine the roasted peppers, walnuts, garlic clove, lemon juice, and cumin. Slowly drizzle in the olive oil and process until it has a smooth consistency similar to hummus, adding more walnuts if it seems thin and you'd like it thicker. Season with salt and freshly ground black pepper and puree one more time. Sprinkle with red chile flakes or Aleppo pepper and serve.

MELITZANOSALATA (GREEK EGGPLANT DIP)

Melitzanosalata, a traditional Greek meze, is something that is always devoured the second it hits the table. Dipping into cold, slippery, mashed-up eggplant heavily seasoned with peppers, herbs, and lemon juice is a delicious and refreshing way to start a meal. It can also be enjoyed as a snack on its own with bread and olives.

Serves 4 to 6

**4 medium Italian eggplants or another variety with few seeds
   (about 2 pounds / 1 kg)
1 medium red bell pepper
1 garlic clove, grated on a Microplane or very finely chopped
1 handful of red onion, finely chopped
Juice of 2 lemons
Extra virgin olive oil
Salt and freshly ground black pepper
2 handfuls flat-leaf parsley, finely chopped**

Preheat the oven to 450°F (230°C). Line a baking sheet with parchment paper.

Prick each eggplant with a fork 3 or 4 times to allow steam to escape while you're cooking it. Place the eggplants and red pepper on the prepared baking sheet and place in the oven. When the eggplant's skin is wrinkled and yields easily to the touch and the red pepper is very soft and charred in spots, 35 to 40 minutes, they are ready. Remove from the oven and cool completely.

Slice the eggplants in half lengthwise and scoop out the flesh. Either chop or mash up any larger pieces. Remove the stem and seeds from the bell pepper and coarsely chop, then add to the eggplant mixture along with the garlic and red onion. Stir in the lemon juice and a nice drizzle of olive oil.

Season generously with salt and freshly ground black pepper. Mix in most of the parsley, then garnish the top with the rest.

SYRIAN BULGUR AND YOGURT WITH BROWN BUTTER PINE NUTS

One of the cookbooks I use the most is *The Aleppo Cookbook* by Marlene Matar, which is a beautiful book filled with Syrian recipes I've incorporated into my cooking. It includes a simple and delicious dip of bulgur wheat soaked in yogurt. I've adapted the recipe by adding olive oil and lemon juice, creating a Syrian version of a Greek tzatziki that combines the best ingredients of both traditions.

The crown finish to this decadent yogurt and bulgur combo is a sprinkle of buttery toasted pine nuts. Serve it with fluffy pita, cucumbers, and olives for a meze spread.

Serves 6 to 8

For the brown butter pine nuts:
1 tablespoon (15 g) butter
¼ cup (45 g) raw pine nuts
Salt

For the bulgur and yogurt:
1 cup (150 g) bulgur wheat
2¼ cups (500 g) plain whole milk Greek yogurt
Juice of 1 lemon
¼ cup (60 ml) extra virgin olive oil
1 garlic clove, finely chopped
Salt and freshly ground black pepper
2 handfuls flat-leaf parsley, finely chopped, plus more for garnish
Red chile flakes

To make the brown butter pine nuts: melt the butter in a small skillet over very low heat. Add the pine nuts and a sprinkle of salt. Toast until they are light golden brown (be patient), 4 to 6 minutes. The butter will foam and turn golden—that's OK. Transfer the pine nuts to a paper towel to drain excess butter.

To make the bulgur and yogurt: place the bulgur in a large bowl and add 2 cups (480 ml) hot water to cover it. Let the bulgur soak for 30 minutes. Drain the water from the bulgur and mix in the yogurt, lemon juice, olive oil, and garlic. Season with salt and freshly ground black pepper. Mix well, then add the parsley. Taste and add more salt if needed.

To serve, garnish with the pine nuts, red chile flakes, chopped parsley, and a drizzle of olive oil.

TZATZIKI

Very Greek, very traditional, tzatziki is basically Greek ketchup, used as a condiment with grilled and braised meats and even as a dip for French fries.

My version of tzatziki has the traditional ingredients of yogurt, cucumber, and olive oil but instead of vinegar I add lemon juice. Instead of a ton of garlic I employ my cousin Margarita's trick—I place whole peeled garlic cloves in the yogurt and remove them a few hours later. It leaves the yummy hint of fresh garlic without the lingering side effects of the full Monty. At times I cannot resist adding lots of fresh mint to this. If you have mint on hand, add it for a fresh and untraditional herbal punch.

½ of a hothouse cucumber (the long kind wrapped in plastic)
2¼ cups (500 g) plain Greek yogurt (I prefer Fage, whole milk yogurt)
¼ cup (60 ml) extra virgin olive oil
Juice of 1 lemon
1 garlic clove, peeled
1 handful mint, freshly chopped (optional)
Salt and freshly ground black pepper

Peel the cucumber and grate it on the large holes of a box grater. Season the grated cucumber with a pinch of salt and place in a fine-mesh sieve over a large bowl. Let sit for 5 minutes, then press out the excess water. You should be left with about ½ cup (85 g) grated cucumber—a little extra or a little less is OK.

Place the grated cucumber in a large bowl and mix in the yogurt, olive oil, and lemon juice. Add a generous pinch of salt and some freshly ground black pepper and stir to combine. Add the garlic clove and let the tzatziki sit, covered, in the refrigerator for 1 to 2 hours (alternatively, chop or finely grate the garlic into the tzatziki). Fish out the garlic, whisk once more, and add in the mint if using. Serve the tzatziki with a drizzle of olive oil on top.

SEASONAL FISH CRUDO WITH BLOOD ORANGES, LIME, AND JALAPEÑO

This is a beautiful recipe (both tasting and looking) that really makes the most of winter produce. The flavor combination of fresh fish with blood oranges, lime, and a kick of jalapeño leaves you wanting more and more.

When you're making a raw fish dish, you always want to ask your fishmonger for sushi-grade fish that is in season, and to remove any skin and bones.

Serves 4 to 6

½ pound (225 g) fresh sushi-grade fish, such as halibut or red snapper, skin and bones removed
3 blood oranges
1 jalapeño, sliced into thin circles
1 lime
Extra virgin olive oil
Salt and freshly ground black pepper
Cilantro leaves for garnish (optional)

Pat the fish dry and slice it as thin as you can. (When the fish is fresh, I find that no matter how you slice it, it comes out delicious. Don't worry about this step too much—just try to get even pieces to fan out on a plate.) Place the sliced fish on a large plate, cover with plastic wrap, and place in the refrigerator.

Slice both ends off of each blood orange and prop them so they are standing up. Cut the orange peel off with a sharp knife starting at the top, following the shape of the orange to the best of your ability. Then slice the oranges into pinwheels (some might fall apart, and that's OK), remove any seeds, and place in a bowl.

To assemble the crudo, remove the fish from the refrigerator and place the blood oranges around and on top of the fish, reserving any juice that remains in the bowl. Scatter the jalapeño slices over the plate.

Slice the lime in half and squeeze the juice over the fish, oranges, and jalapeño. Then drizzle with olive oil and spoon on a bit of the remaining blood orange juice. Finish with a generous sprinkle of salt (make sure every piece of fish gets some), some freshly ground black pepper, and a few cilantro leaves, if using.

SALMON CRUDO WITH LIME ZEST, JALAPEÑO, AND CILANTRO

This dish is adapted from an Alice Waters recipe that changed my life. When I cook for large parties, a successful outcome is often dictated by what can be fresh, beautiful, *and* prepped ahead of time—which can make serving fish a challenge. For this dish, I cut small pieces of sushi-grade salmon (or any other sushi-grade fish) and gently pound it thin with the bottom of a glass. I place the pieces of fish in a single layer on a plate, cover, and refrigerate it until just before serving. This is one of the loveliest ways I know to highlight the flavor and texture of quality salmon, while at the same time creating a flavor bomb of lime, spice, and salt.

Serves 4

½ pound (225 g) sushi-grade salmon, skin and bones removed, preferably center-cut
Extra virgin olive oil
Juice and zest of 2 limes
1 jalapeño, sliced into thin rounds by hand or on a mandoline
Flaky salt, such as Maldon
1 handful cilantro leaves for garnish

Trim the salmon of any fatty tissue and slice into ¼-inch-thick pieces. One at a time, place the pieces on a cutting board and gently pound with the bottom of heavy, flat-bottomed glass until thin. Place the pounded pieces on a dinner plate. Cover the plate with plastic wrap and refrigerate for at least 20 minutes, so the fish gets a nice chill.

When you're ready to serve, drizzle the salmon with a little olive oil and using a microplane or something similar, zest the limes, evenly distributing the zest over the plate of salmon.

Drizzle with the juice of two limes and place a slice of jalapeño on each piece of fish. Sprinkle with salt and garnish with the cilantro leaves.

SALAD

My grandma Macky (she wouldn't let us call her Grandma because it made her feel old) was an antiques dealer, an artist, and a businesswoman, among many other job titles she held. She was fashionable and glamorous, not too into kids and not too into cooking. She loved to drive very fast, like a "bat out of hell" as my dad recalled—an expression that provides a good visual backdrop to her character.

Macky wore lots of costume jewelry and always painted her nails bright red. She would beckon me in the morning, "Mina, come in, I'm about to put *my face on!*"—her expression for putting on makeup—something I patiently watched her do. She'd expertly line her lips and fill them in with lipstick that she blotted on a tissue.

This is all to say that this was not a woman who cooked. She was someone who taught you the art of lip liner.

Macky fully embraced shortcuts and convenience in foods—the complete opposite of my Greek grandmother. She despised cooking and wore this attitude like a badge of honor. And yet everything she made was delicious. At heart, she was incredibly creative and had the ability to apply that creativity in the kitchen in unconventional ways.

I remember frozen pizzas she would top with broccoli and other bits and pieces of vegetables she had lying around. She'd crank the oven and let the pizza get as close as possible to burnt without being *totally* burnt. For dessert we would have bowls of nonfat frozen yogurt topped with nonfat Cool Whip. (It was the late '80s.) Both, in my memory, live in the land of the totally yummy.

What I remember most about Macky is the lunchtime salad that she made almost every day when she got into healthy living and had finally moved away from her Cool Whip days. My cousin Miriam and I would stand on either side of her while she dressed very cold and refreshing bite-size pieces of romaine leaves. She'd drizzle olive oil on the greens, and then she'd drizzle on balsamic vinegar. She'd use her cool silver saltshaker and shake lots of salt and pepper on the salad.

It was *delicious*. Cold, crunchy, salty, sweet, tangy, and every other food word you could think of. It was so simple, but her touch made it so good. We would praise her and tell her that we loved her salad and that we thought she was excellent at making it. Maybe she liked cooking just a little?

My salads are also deceivingly simple and well-dressed. A loving ode to Macky. I like to make salads with different combinations of toasted nuts, seeds, fresh herbs, and occasionally some cheese. My dressing of lemon juice and olive oil is my go-to. I've never had another dressing I liked more, and any variation I make is a riff on that original combination of olive oil, lemon juice, and salt. Once in a blue moon I'll use vinegar, and remember that it, too, is delicious. The biggest tip for a successful salad is to make sure all your ingredients are *dry*—salad spin or wipe off any water so the vegetables are a vehicle for the dressing. Any excess water serves to dilute the dressing and wilt the salad. My other tip is to add an extra sprinkle of salt. It will make all the difference in flavor and turn an otherwise simple salad into a perfect elevated dish.

I usually dress salad with my hands in order to limit the damage on lettuce or shaved vegetables. I dress the salad in the following order: olive oil, then lemon juice, then salt. If it is kale, I like to massage it with olive oil and salt first—in order to break down the leaves a bit—and then add the lemon juice.

A great salad holds your interest with different flavors and textures. It's something to look forward to at every meal or as a meal in itself. Remember that simple food is delicious because there is a greater attention to detail—it's the well-dried greens, the gentle toss, the extra sprinkle of seasoning that make it taste just right.

BABY LETTUCES WITH TOASTED SESAME SEEDS, MINT, AND MEYER LEMON YOGURT

This salad is an ideal platform to showcase any kind of beautiful salad green you can get your hands on. The sesame seeds and yogurt give it a rich and savory flavor, while the mint adds a fresh fragrance. Meyer lemons contribute a nice floral note to the dressing, but regular lemons are just as good. Make sure your salad greens are nicely chilled and very dry! You can add any leafy herb you have on hand, such as basil, cilantro, or parsley, or a bit of all of them.

Serves 6 to 8

For the yogurt dressing:
Zest and juice of 1 organic Meyer lemon
¾ cup (160 g) plain whole milk Greek yogurt
Salt
2 tablespoons water

For the salad:
6 to 8 generous cups (450 g) mixed baby lettuces of your choice
I handful mint leaves or other leafy herb of choice
2 tablespoons sesame seeds, toasted (see page 9)
Salt and freshly ground black pepper

To make the dressing: in a medium bowl, mix the Meyer lemon zest and juice with the yogurt and add a generous pinch of salt. Add the water and whisk to combine.

To assemble the salad: toss the lettuces with a few spoonfuls of dressing, just to barely coat the leaves. You don't want them to get too heavy. Sprinkle with the mint leaves and most of the sesame seeds, reserving a few to garnish the finished salad.

Taste for seasoning and add more salt as needed. Finish the salad by drizzling more dressing over the top and sprinkling the rest of the sesame seeds over the lettuces. Finish with freshly ground black pepper.

CARROT SALAD WITH TOASTED SEEDS AND NUTS

A bright rainbow of colors, this salad is tasty, crunchy, and relatively easy to prepare. What I love most about this salad is that it can be dressed ahead of time, as the carrots can withstand the dressing—and it can sit eye-poppingly on the table ready to go. I like to freshly toast seeds I have in my pantry—two of my favorites are sesame and pumpkin. You can add any toasted nuts you like, but if you use pistachios, keep them raw to retain their bright green color and delicate flavor.

Serves 6 to 8

8 medium carrots (1½ pounds / 680 g), a mix of orange, yellow, and purple if you can find them, peeled and sliced into thin rounds by hand or on a mandoline
Juice of 3 lemons
¼ cup (35 g) sesame seeds or pumpkin seeds or a mix, toasted (see page 9)
¼ cup (30 g) raw pistachios, or any other nut, toasted (see page 9)
Extra virgin olive oil
Salt and freshly ground black pepper
2 handfuls mint leaves, bigger leaves torn in half

To assemble the salad: in a large bowl, toss the carrot slices with the lemon juice, a large pinch of salt, and lots of freshly ground black pepper. Add half of the toasted seeds and half of the chopped nuts and toss with your hands to combine.

Spread the salad over a large serving platter and scatter the remaining seeds and nuts on top. Drizzle generously with olive oil, another sprinkle of salt and freshly ground black pepper, and finish with the mint leaves to serve.

STUFFED AVOCADOS WITH RED CABBAGE, RADISHES, AND CILANTRO

This is a lush and rich salad served in the avocado itself that is fun to scoop out on your plate and eat with crispy Arctic Char (page 66) or Black Bean Stew Topped with Feta, Cilantro, and Jalapeños (page 119). I like that my guests feel relaxed knowing that they will get an entire half of an avocado, covered in crunchy cabbage and radish, to themselves. This dish is an instant crowd pleaser.

Serves 6

3 ripe Hass avocados, cut in half and pit removed
Juice of 2 or 3 limes
Half medium-large head red cabbage, cored and shaved thinly
1 bunch radishes, trimmed and cut into rounds or half-moons
2 handfuls cilantro, coarsely chopped
¼ cup of toasted pumpkin seeds (see page 9)
Salt and freshly ground black pepper

Run your knife across the avocado halves to make cross-hatches and form 1-inch cubes (keeping them in the shell), being careful to not cut through the skin. Season generously with salt and squeeze some lime juice on each avocado half. Toss the cabbage with the radishes and cilantro, reserving a handful of cilantro for garnish. Add the rest of the lime juice and the pumpkin seeds and toss to combine. Season generously with salt and freshly ground black pepper.

To serve, place the avocados on a platter and top with a handful of the cabbage, radish, pumpkin seeds, and cilantro salad. Sprinkle with remaining cilantro and some freshly ground black pepper.

TOMATO SALAD WITH TAHINI AND MINT

I saw this salad on the menu of one of my favorite restaurants in Brooklyn a few years ago and thought . . . tomatoes? With tahini? I hesitantly ordered it, and to this day, it remains one of my very favorite salads to eat and re-create. Seasonal tomatoes, full of flavor, pair perfectly with a super lemony tahini and fresh mint. It is so easy, so beautiful, and very tasty.

Serves 4 to 6

For the tahini:
½ cup (120 ml) tahini
Juice of 2 lemons
⅓ cup (80 ml) water, plus more if needed
Salt

For the salad:
4 medium to large heirloom tomatoes, cut into bite-size wedges
1 handful of cherry tomatoes, cut in half
Juice of ½ a lemon
Extra virgin olive oil
Salt and freshly ground black pepper
2 handfuls fresh mint leaves

To make the tahini: in a medium bowl, whisk the tahini with the lemon juice and water. Add more water as necessary to reach a thick but spreadable consistency, like whipped cream. Season with salt to taste.

To assemble the salad: spread the tahini on a large platter in a thick layer and nestle the wedges of heirloom tomatoes on top of it. Scatter the cherry tomatoes over the tahini and heirloom tomatoes. Squeeze the lemon half over the tomatoes and drizzle the salad generously with olive oil. Sprinkle with salt and freshly ground black pepper and scatter the mint leaves over the salad to serve.

KALE SALAD WITH FETA, DILL, AND TOASTED SEEDS

This is a hearty salad that has so much herby flavor, soft creaminess from the feta, and savory crunch from the pumpkin and sesame seeds that I think it deserves a gold medal in the still-unheard-of Salad Olympics.

It stands alone as dinner (maybe with a fried egg), and it is a great salad for a BBQ or dinner party because you can dress it ahead of time and have it ready to serve.

Serves 4 to 6

6 cups (400 g) lacinto kale (about 2 bunches)
Extra virgin olive oil
Juice of 1 lemon
½ cup (100 g) good-quality feta, crumbled
2 handfuls fresh dill, coarsely chopped
¼ cup (30 g) pumpkin seeds, toasted (see page 9)
2 tablespoons sesame seeds, toasted (see page 9)
Salt and freshly ground black pepper

Cut out the thick middle rib of the kale leaves or tear it off with your hands. Layer a few kale leaves on top of each other and cut into bite-size pieces. Repeat until all the kale is done.

Put the kale in a serving bowl and massage it with enough olive oil to coat each leaf. Add the lemon juice and a sprinkle of salt, massage it in, and toss again. Taste for seasoning and add more lemon juice and salt if needed.

When you are ready to serve, gently toss the feta, dill, and toasted pumpkin and sesame seeds with the kale. Finish with some freshly ground black pepper.

CACIO E PEPE–INSPIRED KALE SALAD

This is my version of having the idea of a decadent pasta, in salad form.

It has the flavor components of a *cacio e pepe*, set against the backdrop of a hearty forest of green kale. The kale stands up to the challenge, providing a healthy vehicle for the tangy salty cheese, crunchy hazelnuts, and spicy black pepper.

Serves 4 to 6

6 cups (400 g) lacinato or curly green kale (about 2 bunches)
Extra virgin olive oil
Juice and zest of 1 lemon
Salt and freshly ground black pepper
½ cup (40 g) grated pecorino cheese
½ cup (65 g) hazelnuts, toasted (see page 9) and chopped

Cut out the thick middle rib of the kale leaves or tear it off with your hands. Layer a few kale leaves on top of each other and cut into bite-size pieces. Repeat until all the kale is done. (Alternatively, you can cut the kale into ribbon-size pieces for a "pasta" look.)

Put the kale in a serving bowl and massage it with enough olive oil to coat each leaf.

Add the lemon zest, lemon juice, a sprinkle of salt, and lots of freshly ground black pepper.

When you are ready to serve, toss the kale with most of the cheese and most of the hazelnuts and garnish with the rest. Finish with freshly ground black pepper and serve.

SHAVED FENNEL WITH BLISTERED GOLDEN RAISINS AND PISTACHIO DRESSING

This salad was invented when I was craving a richer salad, almost like a coleslaw, but wanted to skip the heaviness mayonnaise can sometimes create. The fennel here has a cold, refreshing crunch and holds up well to the sweet raisins and creamy dressing that comes from blending the pistachios with olive oil and lemon juice. It is a lovely refined salad and also a welcome alternative to a traditional coleslaw.

Serves 4 to 6

For the salad:
3 to 4 large fennel bulbs, trimmed of fronds
⅓ cup (50 g) golden raisins
Extra virgin olive oil
¼ cup (30 g) raw pistachios, chopped
2 handfuls flat-leaf parsley, chopped
Salt and freshly ground black pepper

For the dressing:
¼ cup (30 g) raw pistachios
⅓ cup (80 ml) extra virgin olive oil
Zest of 1 lemon
Juice of 2 lemons
Salt and freshly ground black pepper

Shave or slice the fennel as a whole bulb crosswise (so you get nice circles or half-circles of fennel). Place in a bowl, cover with a damp towel, and place in the refrigerator.

Set a medium skillet over medium heat and add the raisins and enough olive oil to barely coat them. Add a generous sprinkle of salt. Cook until the raisins puff up and blister a bit and get a little golden-brown color. Remove from the heat and set aside.

To make the dressing: combine the pistachios, olive oil, lemon zest, lemon juice, and a pinch of salt and freshly ground black pepper in a blender. Blitz until nice and smooth, adding a little water if it is too thick. Taste for seasoning and add more lemon juice and/or salt to get a nice tangy dressing.

To assemble the salad: toss the fennel with half of the dressing and serve the rest on the side. Add the chopped pistachios, raisins, and most of the chopped parsley. Garnish with the remaining parsley and a sprinkle of salt and freshly ground pepper and serve.

CUCUMBER SALAD WITH TOASTED SESAME SEEDS, DILL, AND PARSLEY

Warm Up, an infamous yearly music festival at PS1, was our first introduction to cooking for thousands of people. Every Saturday of our first summer at PS1, we planned the menu around food that could be made ahead of time but still stay fresh and delicious. We paired this salad with Santorini Dogs (page 87) and Oven Braised Chickpeas with Orange Zest and Garlic Breadcrumbs (page 114), our version of street food. Quick and tasty, it's food meant to hit the spot and inspire you to stay a little longer.

This salad is close to a crunchy and refreshing quick pickle. The dill and parsley hold up to the dressing and don't lose their vibrant green color, while the sesame seeds add little pops of toasty deliciousness. It is one of the few times I like vinegar better than lemon juice because the cucumber really needs the robust acidity it provides. The cucumber absorbs the vinegar and salt after a while, and it needs to be seasoned a second time to pack the proper punch. Keep that in mind and taste right before serving.

I like using a seasonal mix of cucumber varieties, but any kind you have on hand will be great.

Serves 6 to 8

3 large cucumbers, sliced into ¼-inch-thick half-moons
   (or 8 small cucumbers, cut into ¼-inch-thick rounds)
2 handfuls flat-leaf parsley, finely chopped
2 handfuls dill, finely chopped
¼ cup (40 g) sesame seeds, toasted (see page 9)
Extra virgin olive oil
Red wine vinegar
Salt and freshly ground black pepper

In a large bowl, toss the cucumbers with the parsley, dill, and sesame seeds. Drizzle lightly with olive oil, then drizzle with enough vinegar so it is extra tangy. Generously salt and pepper the salad.

Chill the salad for up to 2 hours and then taste and re-season before serving. Don't be surprised at how much seasoning you will need to make this salad really vibrant.

Variation: add 1 watermelon radish, thinly sliced into half-moons, for a pop of color (serve immediately for this version).

GEORGIAN-INSPIRED GREEK SALAD WITH HERBS

Georgia is close to my heart because my great-grandmother was a Pontic Greek, an ethnically Greek group that lived on the shores of the Black Sea of Georgia. I had this salad at a little Georgian restaurant when I was cooking at the Garage Museum of Contemporary Art in Moscow a few years ago. It was what I know to be a traditional Greek salad, but with the revolutionary addition of cilantro, mint, and basil. You'll assemble the salad in layers, seasoning each layer with salt and a little squeeze of lemon juice as you go.

I ate this salad with a dish called *khachapuri,* a freshly baked bread boat with a cracked egg in the center covered in hot butter. Breaking off pieces of the fresh bread and dipping it into the runny center of the yolk covered in butter alternating with forkfuls of the fresh and herby salad was something close to bliss. Try it with any combination of green herbs—fresh oregano, tarragon, and parsley to name a few.

Serves 6 to 8

4 medium to large tomatoes, preferably heirloom, sliced into wedges
4 Persian cucumbers, sliced into ¼-inch rounds
1 medium green bell pepper, cored and sliced
Half small red onion, sliced into thin half-moons
1 handful basil, chopped
1 handful mint, whole leaves intact or torn
1 handful cilantro
½ pound (225 g) good-quality feta, preferably Greek
Generous pinch of dried oregano (about 1 teaspoon)
1 handful kalamata olives
1 small handful capers, rinsed
Salt
Juice of 1 lemon
Extra virgin olive oil

Arrange the tomatoes on the bottom of a large bowl. Season with salt and a little lemon juice. Add the cucumbers, green pepper, and onion and sprinkle with salt and lemon juice again. Scatter the basil, mint, and cilantro over the vegetables. Place the hunk of feta on top. Sprinkle the salad with the dried oregano and scatter the olives and capers around the feta. Drizzle with a generous pour of olive oil and finish with another sprinkle of salt and another squeeze of lemon. At the table, break the chunks of feta up into the salad, toss everything together, and serve.

RADICCHIO AND CHICORY SALAD WITH TOASTED HAZELNUTS, MINT, AND BUTTERMILK DRESSING

This is our fancy cold-weather salad at the café, and it's a true beauty in both flavor and looks. In fall and winter, pastel-colored radicchios come into season. We toss baby pink, light green, and red-colored bitter greens with a slightly sweet, tangy, and rich buttermilk dressing, then add a crunch of toasted hazelnuts and fresh herbal mint leaves. For the fruit component, I like to use what's in season—sliced pears or apples in the fall and oranges in the winter. This is truly a salad that leaves you wanting . . . more salad, please!

Serves 6 to 8

For the buttermilk dressing:
½ cup (120 ml) buttermilk, preferably full-fat
2 tablespoons red wine vinegar
¼ cup (60 ml) extra virgin olive oil
1 tablespoon honey
Salt and freshly ground black pepper

For the salad:
6 generous cups (1 pound / 450 g) mixed radicchio and endive,
   such as Castelfranco and Chioggia varieties
⅓ cup (40 g) hazelnuts, toasted (see page 9) and chopped
1 handful mint leaves
1 tart apple or Bartlett pear, cored and sliced, or 2 oranges
   (preferably blood or Cara Cara oranges), segmented
Salt and freshly ground black pepper

To make the dressing: whisk or shake all the ingredients together in a bowl or jar. Taste for seasoning and add more salt and freshly ground black pepper if needed.

To assemble the salad: in a large bowl, toss the radicchio and endive leaves with just enough dressing to coat each leaf. Be gentle and preferably use your hands to toss the salad. Sprinkle with the hazelnuts and mint leaves and tuck in the fruit. Drizzle more dressing over the salad, sprinkle with salt and freshly ground black pepper, and serve.

FISH

Nostalgia: a sentimental longing for the past, coming from the Greek nostos, *to "return home" and* algos, *for "pain."*

The rituals that define my idea of family and home are many. They are the archives that live in the recesses of my mind, called upon involuntarily, usually through smell, sound, and a change in the weather.

My parents met when they were in college—my father, on a study abroad trip to Greece; my mother, a medical student in Athens. Eventually, they came to settle in Boston, and long summer trips to Greece became an integral part of my existence.

My mother would start packing a month in advance, carefully laying out neatly folded clothes and gifts. Ralph Lauren shirts requested by a cousin, Hugo Boss button-downs for another, perfume—Nina Ricci, L'Air du Temps—for my grandmother and her sisters.

The anticipation was palpable. It was the most joyous and exciting time of the year. We would touch down after the long flight and descend the stairs from the airplane into the dry heat of Greece, my mother exhausted but beaming.

We'd arrive at my grandmother's house and find her in the kitchen. After brief and tearful kisses, she'd heat up a frying pan with olive oil and flour fish called *gavros,* a type of small anchovy common in the Mediterranean Sea. I would watch her dip the tip of her finger in water and gently press the tails of three or four fish together, so they formed a fan, and drop them into the hot olive oil. The smell of fried fish permeated the house and veranda, and soon we would sit down to one of my favorite summertime meals of fried *gavros,* boiled *horta* (greens), and Greek salad complete with thick pieces of fresh bread to sop up the olive oil.

Greek women have a trait I envy deeply. They can sit quietly, make no mess or fuss, and eat an entire fish—every single part—so that it looks like a cartoon after a cat dips a fish down its throat and brings out the skeleton. Eating *gavros* with my grandmother was always a test of my Greekness: *could I eat the whole thing? Head, bones, and tail? But the bones are so small! Eat bread if a bone gets stuck in your throat. The head is good for you! Full of vitamins.* And so on and so forth—an evaluation of how much of America had permeated into my being since the previous summer.

Fish to me is the spirit of summertime and a nebulous test of my identity. *Can I eat the whole fish? Head, bones, and tail?* It involuntarily reminds me of who I am—and yes, I can eat the whole fish (if I really try). It reminds me of that journey I took with my mom every summer and the alluring smell that greeted us when my yiayia opened her door to welcome us back.

WHITE ANCHOVIES WITH LEMON, CHILE, AND PARSLEY

This dish is a nod to the fried fresh anchovies called *gavros* that my yiayia would make (and which are impossible to find in NYC!). It is a favorite at the café, and an anchovy lover's dream. It hits all the satisfying notes you want out of the tiny fish—namely its delightful fishiness balanced with the zip of lemon juice, a little spice, and a fresh herb. This dish only works with lovely cured white anchovies, also known by their Spanish name of *boquerones*. Serve this as a meze or side alongside Oven-Braised Lentils (page 126) and Spigarello (page 162).

Serves 4

12 white anchovies (*boquerones*)
Extra virgin olive oil
Juice of 1 lemon
Kosher salt
Red chile flakes
A few leaves fresh flat-leaf parsley

Place the anchovies on a plate skin-side up. Drizzle with olive oil and lemon juice, and finish with a sprinkle of salt and red chile flakes. Garnish with parsley leaves and serve.

ARCTIC CHAR WITH CRISPY CUMIN CRUST

My mom likes to overcook fish. When I think about it, so did my yiayia. They both leave fish in the oven or on the grill forever, completely disregarding the idea of cooking fish "just so." I think their influence gave me the confidence to develop this recipe and harness the power of "overcooked" to my advantage. The fish ends up absorbing the olive oil and lemon juice, creating juicy, flavorful mouthfuls.

I crank the oven high and cover the skin side of the fish with a paste of lemon juice, oregano, cumin, and salt. Then I roast it until the skin is crackly and crisp. To serve, I separate the fish from the skin and break it up into pieces. I drizzle it with olive oil and lemon juice and tuck in the pieces of crispy skin throughout.

Serves 4

Juice of 2 lemons, divided
2 tablespoons ground cumin
1 tablespoon dried oregano
1 tablespoon extra virgin olive oil
1 side arctic char (about 2 pounds / 1 kg)
Salt and freshly ground black pepper

Preheat the oven to 450°F (230°C) and line a baking sheet with parchment paper.

Make the cumin paste by stirring together the juice of 1 lemon, the cumin, oregano, and olive oil in a small bowl.

Spoon the paste on both sides of the arctic char and generously sprinkle with salt and freshly ground pepper. Place skin-side down on the prepared baking sheet.

Roast for 20 to 25 minutes, until you can lift the fish and see that the skin is crisp.

Remove the fish from its skin and break up the flesh into chunks using a knife or your fingers. Place on a platter and drizzle with more olive oil and the juice of the second lemon. Break the crispy skin into pieces and tuck around the fish to serve.

OLIVE OIL–POACHED FISH WITH CARAMELIZED ONIONS AND CHICKPEAS

I developed this recipe when I was serving fish family-style for a wedding. I needed a fish I could prepare a few hours ahead of time, so I could heat, plate, and garnish it quickly before serving. I decided to poach the fish in olive oil and top it with a sweet, crispy onion-chickpea mixture for a dish that is both light and filling.

I managed to combine lots of my favorite ingredients into this recipe, but you can certainly customize it to your preference. Try infusing the oil with different herbs, hot chiles, or a few garlic cloves, or serving it with a lightly dressed salad of various fresh herbs, such as mint, cilantro, and basil to garnish the dish.

Serves 4 to 6

For the fish:
2 cups (480 ml) extra virgin olive oil
2 bay leaves
4 sprigs thyme
6 strips lemon peel (from 1 lemon)
2 pounds (1 kg) white fish, such as cod, black cod, or hake
Salt and freshly ground black pepper

For the caramelized onions and chickpeas:
2 tablespoons (30 g) butter
2 medium yellow onions, cut into ¼-inch half-moons
1 (15-ounce / 439-g) can chickpeas, rinsed well, or 1¾ cups soaked (see page 108) and cooked chickpeas
Extra virgin olive oil
Zest and juice of 2 lemons
Salt and freshly ground black pepper
1 handful flat-leaf parsley, chopped, for garnish

To make the fish: in a medium skillet, combine the olive oil, bay leaves, thyme, and lemon peel and heat over low heat for about 10 minutes, until the oil becomes aromatic.

Cut the fish into 2- to 3-inch chunks and sprinkle generously with salt and freshly ground black pepper. Add it to the olive oil and poach the fish over medium-low heat, occasionally spooning hot oil over the top, until it is just falling apart, about 6 minutes. Remove from the heat and set aside. Keep in mind the fish will continue to cook as it sits in the olive oil. The fish can be poached up to 6 hours ahead of time. Cool it submerged in the oil, cover, and keep in the refrigerator. Reheat over low heat until just warmed through.

To make the caramelized onions and chickpeas: in a large skillet, melt the butter in the olive oil over medium heat. Add the onions and a generous sprinkle of salt and cook until the onions start to soften and get some crispy golden-brown color, about 5 minutes. Add the chickpeas and, if the mixture seems dry, a little more olive oil. Add the lemon zest and cook until the chickpeas are heated through and a little crispy, about 3 more minutes. Remove from the heat, add the lemon juice, and toss to combine. Taste for seasoning and add more salt if needed and lots of freshly ground black pepper.

Using a slotted spoon, remove the fish from the oil and place on a large shallow platter. Spoon the caramelized onions and chickpeas over the fish. Finish with the parsley and serve.

TUNA SALAD WITH FENNEL, APPLE, AND PARSLEY

One of the most defining moments of my childhood was witnessing what each of my parents could do with a can of tuna fish.

My Greek mom would open up a can, drizzle it with olive oil and lemon juice, and eat it without any additional accompaniment. My dad, a Jewish man from Ohio, gave it the traditional tuna salad treatment with celery and mayonnaise.

This simple lunch is inspired by both of them—it's my Jewish-Greek tuna salad. It's lighter and more refreshing than a traditional tuna salad, with the fennel and apples to replace the celery and add a satisfying crunch. I like serving this dish alongside French Lentils with Caramelized Fennel and Golden Raisins (page 125), on top of simply dressed greens, or on toast drizzled with olive oil.

Serves 2 to 4

2 (5-ounce) cans tuna, preferably olive oil–packed
1 large fennel bulb, trimmed of fronds, cored and diced
1 Granny Smith or Pink Lady apple, cored and diced
Juice of 2 lemons
Extra virgin olive oil
Salt and freshly ground black pepper
1 handful flat-leaf parsley, finely chopped

Drain the cans of tuna and flake the fish into a large bowl. Add the fennel, apple, lemon juice, a generous drizzle of olive oil, and a generous sprinkle of salt and freshly ground black pepper. Toss to combine. Add the parsley and toss one more time.

CRISPY OCTOPUS WITH OREGANO

Crispy octopus is a seaside Greek taverna favorite. After simmering the octopus in water and aromatics, it is finished on the grill, with its crispy tendrils covered in lots of oregano, salt, and—depending on your preference—red wine vinegar or lemon juice.

I re-created this dish for indoor cooking when that seaside taverna was instead a New York apartment. You do need a gas stove, some metal tongs, and a vigilant attitude to cook this magical dish (and not burn it). It doesn't disappoint, and it will transport you right to that island happy place. For authenticity, serve with wooden toothpicks and a little ouzo over ice with a splash of water.

Serves 4 to 6

2 to 3 pounds (1 to 1.5 kg) octopus, cleaned
2 bay leaves
10 black peppercorns
¼ cup (60 ml) red wine vinegar
Salt
Extra virgin olive oil
Juice of 2 lemons
Dried oregano

Place the octopus, bay leaves, peppercorns, vinegar, and a generous pinch of salt in a medium-size pot and add just enough water to cover the octopus. Bring to a boil over high heat, then reduce the heat to maintain a simmer and simmer for 30 to 40 minutes, until tender. Remove from the liquid and cool.

Separate the octopus head from the legs and discard. Divide the legs for grilling. Turn a gas burner to medium-high. Place 1 or 2 octopus pieces right on the metal part of the burner. They will pop a bit and stick to the burner.

You will know they are done when they don't stick anymore and you can remove them easily. Repeat with the rest of the octopus. (Alternatively, you can sear the octopus on a lightly oiled very hot cast-iron skillet or other pan for about 3 minutes, until it's nice and crispy.)

Cut the octopus into bite-size pieces and drizzle with olive oil and the lemon juice. Sprinkle with salt and oregano.

SALMON IN LETTUCE LEAVES WITH HERBS AND CITRUS CREMA

This light meal combines beautiful bright pink salmon, fresh herbs, and tangy lime crema all wrapped up in a blanket of pretty red lettuce leaves. You can pre-assemble a platter of them to serve, or lay out all the fillings and let your guests have fun making their own. This is perfect accompanied with Stuffed Avocados with Red Cabbage, Radishes, and Cilantro (page 44) for a colorful summertime meal.

Serves 6 to 8

1 side salmon, preferably wild (about 3 pounds / 1.5 kg)
Extra virgin olive oil
1 (8-ounce / 225-g) container sour cream
Zest and juice of 3 limes
Salt and freshly ground black pepper
2 heads red leaf lettuce, trimmed of outer leaves, inner leaves separated
3 cups (60 g) mixed leafy herbs, such as mint, basil, cilantro, and parsley

Preheat the oven to 400°F (200°C).

Place the salmon on a baking sheet and use a paring knife to make 3 or 4 incisions about 1 inch deep, spaced 2 inches apart on the thicker half of the fish. Drizzle with a bit of olive oil and sprinkle generously with salt and freshly ground black pepper.

Roast in the oven for 12 to 15 minutes, until the salmon is cooked but still a bit pink in the center.

To make the crema, in a medium bowl, whisk the sour cream with the lime zest, lime juice, and salt. It should be very bright and tart.

Arrange the lettuce leaves on a large platter with the herbs. Serve with the fish and crema on the side or fill each lettuce leaf with a bit of salmon, crema, and herbs.

BACALIAROS TIGANITOS (FRIED SALT COD)

I beg my mother to make me this dish every time I come home. It's my greatest comfort. Frying is no small task; it's something you do once in a while because it is going to be worth it and you really want to give someone you love something tasty to eat.

This battered and fried salt cod is traditionally served with vinegared beets (page 168) and tangy garlicky Skordalia (page 181). Bright red sweet beets, salty, crunchy cod, and a mess of spicy and garlicky potatoes is one happy marriage.

This batter can also be used with any white fish you want to fry—it comes together easily and creates a light and airy coating.

Serves 6 to 8

1 side salt cod (2 to 2½ pounds / 1 kg), cut into 3-inch pieces
2 cups (240 g) all-purpose flour
2 teaspoons salt
1 cup (240 ml) seltzer water
Canola oil for frying
Lemon wedges for serving

Soak the cod in a bowl of cold water for 8 to 10 hours, changing the water three times.

Drain the cod, pat dry, and set aside on a plate.

Mix the flour and salt together in a shallow bowl, then add the seltzer.

In a large skillet, heat 3 inches of canola oil over medium-high heat. The oil is hot enough when you drop a little batter in and it sizzles. (Remove it before frying the fish.)

Dip the fish pieces in the batter and gently place 5 or 6 pieces at a time in the hot oil. Fry until golden brown, turning the pieces with a fork slightly so they are loose in the oil and can brown evenly. If the oil starts to splatter, turn the heat down slightly.

Remove the fish with a slotted spoon onto a drying rack or plate lined with paper towels to absorb the excess oil. You can keep the cooked fish warm on a baking sheet in a 300°F (150°C) oven while you fry the rest of the fish. Serve immediately with lemon wedges.

CRISPY BROOK TROUT

I enjoy any fresh, local fish, but I especially love the trout available at my farmers' market in New York City. Trout is native to eastern North America and has a light pink flesh and mild flavor. It's easy to cook and makes a perfect summer meal. This technique of cooking the fish is so easy—just lay it skin-side down on a hot pan—and the result is perfectly cooked fish with super crispy skin.

Serves 4

4 whole brook trout (about 2 pounds / 1 kg), cleaned and butterflied, head
    and tail intact (a good substitute is skin-on arctic char or red snapper fillets)
Salt and freshly ground black pepper
Extra virgin olive oil
1 lemon, cut into wedges, for serving

Generously salt and pepper the skin side of the trout and set aside.

Heat two medium to large skillets over medium-high heat with enough olive oil in each to completely coat the bottom of the pans. When some smoke is coming off the pans, add two brook trout, skin-side down, to each pan. Sprinkle just a little salt on the flesh side of the fish and sear for about 6 minutes, until when you pull the tail the fish easily comes off the pan. Lower the heat and cover with a lid of aluminum foil. Cook until the top of the fish is no longer pink and cooked through, another 3 to 4 minutes.

Remove from the heat. Serve the fish whole, straight from the pan, with lemon wedges.

MEAT

When I first met Alex (who is also half-Greek), we made and rolled over two hundred meatballs for a gallery dinner in my tiny kitchen nestled in my very small apartment. We sat at the tables for hours, rolling meatballs we would eventually cook and cover in a lemony Greek sauce called *avgolemono* to re-create a dish called *yourvalakia*, which was Alex's favorite as a child, the food he would always request when he would go home to see his mother.

We stacked the meatballs into a huge pyramid on my kitchen table, swearing that we would think it through next time, do a braise, make the meatballs for a smaller dinner. But the truth is I appreciated the time it took to roll the meatballs because I wanted to hang out with him as long as possible.

It's been years since that dinner, but we can't escape our fate, so it seems. Alex and I have ended up making these meatballs for various events and parties throughout the years—the allure of them ends up being all-consuming, and it makes one forget past traumas of long meatball-rolling evenings.

I like to cook meat once in a while and take my time with it, remembering when I wanted time to go slower, when I wanted to have another hundred meatballs to roll. I believe cooking meat should be sacrificial, special, and not an everyday practice. Many of the recipes in this section of the book stretch a meat-based ingredient to go further by adding rice or a sauce, turning it into a taco filling, or roasting it with vegetables. All time-honored techniques of stretching a precious material in order to feed more people.

I like meat cooked simply, falling off the bone after long hours in the oven. I like it seared or roasted with a crispy salty crust and squeezing lemon over it, which takes it to a whole new level of deliciousness—something very Greek and not common in the United States.

What I enjoy making the most these days is *biftekia*, a Greek dish of ground beef that is sharp with the flavors of lemon and oregano. It also happens to be our son Apollo's favorite dinner. A *bifteki* is also the shape of a rather large meatball, which means . . . less rolling.

YOURVALAKIA (MEATBALLS WITH RICE AND PARSLEY IN LEMON BROTH)

This dish is a simple and traditional Greek stew of meatballs studded with rice in a silky, lemony *avgolemono* sauce. A warm bowl of this soup, paired with fresh bread and a salad, is just the thing I crave on a cold winter day.

Serves 4

For the meatballs:
1 pound (500 g) ground beef
¼ cup (50 g) uncooked long-grain rice,
   such as jasmine or Carolina, rinsed
1 medium yellow onion, grated on the large holes
   of a box grater and juice gently squeezed out
2 handfuls flat-leaf parsley, finely chopped,
   plus more for garnish

For the *avgolemono*:
1 egg, at room temperature
Juice of 2 lemons
Salt and freshly ground black pepper

To make the meatballs: in a large bowl, mix the ground beef with the rice, onion, and parsley. Add a generous pinch of salt and a few grinds of black pepper. Knead briefly, until all the ingredients come together and are nicely incorporated. Roll the mixture into meatballs a little larger than a golf ball. Set on a plate and put in the refrigerator for 20 minutes (this helps set the meatball).

In a medium pot, bring 4 cups (946 ml) water to a boil over high heat. Reduce the heat to medium-low and gently add the meatballs. The water should come about 1 inch over the top of the meatballs; add more warm water if necessary. Simmer for 30 to 35 minutes, until the meatballs are just cooked through and the rice is tender. Turn off the heat and prepare the *avgolemono*.

To make the *avgolemono*: in a medium bowl, whisk the egg with the lemon juice and very slowly add a ladle of broth, whisking the whole time. Whisk in another two ladles of broth, then slowly drizzle the *avgolemono* back into the pot with the meatballs, stirring the entire time. Turn the heat back on to low and stir until it just starts to simmer. The broth should be velvety and thick like the consistency of heavy cream. Turn the heat off once again and taste for seasoning, adding salt and freshly ground black pepper as needed. Garnish with parsley and serve.

SANTORINI DOGS

This is Alex's invention of an American souvlaki that substitutes a hot dog for the traditional seasoned shaved pork. The hot dogs are served in a potato bun and topped with tzatziki, diced tomatoes, onions, parsley, and a dash of cayenne pepper. It might sound crazy, but it is insanely delicious, and we served them at PS1 Warm Up to thousands of happy hot dog eaters.

Serves 12

12 beef hot dogs, grilled or boiled
12 potato buns
Tzatziki (page 30)
2 medium tomatoes, diced
1 small red onion, sliced into thin half-moons
1 bunch flat-leaf parsley, finely chopped
Cayenne pepper (optional)

Place the hot dogs in the buns and top first with the tzatziki (about 2 tablespoons), then some diced tomatoes, onion, and parsley. Finish with a dusting of cayenne, or *kaftero*—something that burns—for a little heat, if you like.

PULLED CHICKEN WITH CORIANDER AND CUMIN

I often make this chicken as a filling for tacos, simply topped with shaved green cabbage, jalapeños and lime, or to serve alongside black beans and rice. It's bright and spicy from the cumin and coriander, and the meat falls apart while simmering in the aromatic juices.

Serves 4 to 6

¼ cup (60 g) butter
Extra virgin olive oil
2 medium yellow onions, sliced into half-moons
4 garlic cloves, chopped
2 heaping tablespoons ground cumin
2 teaspoons ground coriander
2 boneless skinless chicken breast halves (about 1½ pounds / 680 g)
Juice of 2 limes
Salt and freshly ground black pepper
1 handful cilantro, chopped, for garnish

In a medium skillet, melt the butter with a generous drizzle of olive oil over medium-low heat. Add the onions, garlic, and a pinch of salt and cook until the onions start to soften, about 5 minutes. Add the cumin and coriander and cook for 1 minute more. Add the chicken breast to the pan, moving the onions so you can nestle the chicken in between. Add enough water to barely cover the chicken.

Bring the liquid to a boil, then reduce the heat to low and cover the pan with a lid slightly tilted so that the steam can evaporate. Cook the chicken for 60 minutes, flipping halfway through, until it is cooked through and the water has reduced to a delicious sauce.

Remove the chicken from the pan and place it on a cutting board. Using your hands or a fork, shred the chicken breasts (the chicken should shred easily; if it is still tough, add it back to the pan and cook for 10 more minutes) and place them back into the pan, adding more water to keep it juicy and loose. Add the lime juice and taste for seasoning. Add salt, freshly ground black pepper, and more olive oil as needed. Garnish with cilantro and serve.

SALTY ROASTED WHOLE CHICKEN WITH OREGANO

This recipe yields a chicken that is juicy inside and salty and crispy on the outside. What really makes the difference in preparing a perfectly roasted chicken are these three things:

1) Using a well-dried chicken.
2) Roasting it on a baking sheet with low sides (i.e., a cookie sheet).
3) Sprinkling it with a generous amount of kosher salt and dusting it with lots of dried oregano.

Everything else, as far as I am concerned, is an extra.

To serve, I like to carve the chicken and place all the pieces back in the pan it was roasted in to catch all the salty crispy bits. Squeezing a wedge of lemon over your piece of chicken is very Greek and the perfect way to add a bright zip of lemon to cut the richness of the crispy skin.

Serves 4

1 whole chicken (3 to 4 pounds / 1.5 to 1.75 kg)
Kosher salt and freshly ground black pepper
Dried oregano, preferably Greek
1 lemon, cut into wedges

Preheat the oven to 450°F (230°C).

Pat the chicken dry on the inside and outside and generously sprinkle both inside and outside with salt, freshly ground black pepper, and oregano.

Place on a baking sheet and roast in the oven for 1 hour. Remove the chicken and let it rest for 10 to 15 minutes. Carve the chicken and place the chicken pieces back in the roasting pan. Serve with lemon wedges.

APPLE CIDER AND PEPPERCORN BRAISED PORK SHOULDER

When I get in the mood for a rich and flavorful braised meat on a brisk autumn day, this is the dish I make. The combination of apple cider vinegar and apple cider create a delicious sweet and sour sauce for the fall-off-the-bone tender pork.

The braised peppercorns burst in your mouth, having softened in the long cooking process, and add a welcome spiciness. It is an addition I learned about after eating lots of adobo from the hands of my friend Daphne Lopez, who taught me everything I know about Filipino food.

I serve this dish with thinly shredded cabbage dressed simply with olive oil and lemon juice, steamed rice, and hot sauce.

Serves 4 to 6

1 (3- to 4-pound / 1.5- to 1.75-kg) bone-in pork shoulder
2 garlic cloves, thinly sliced
2 large yellow or white onions, cut into thin half-moons
2 bay leaves
1 tablespoon whole black peppercorns
1 cup (240 ml) apple cider vinegar
½ cup (120 ml) apple cider
1 tablespoon light or dark brown sugar
Salt and freshly ground black pepper

Preheat the oven to 350°F (180°C). Pat the pork shoulder dry.

Cut 1-inch-deep slits randomly throughout the pork shoulder and stuff a few slices of garlic into them. In a medium Dutch oven, combine the onions, bay leaves, and peppercorns. Sprinkle the pork shoulder generously with salt and freshly ground black pepper and place on top of the bed of onions. Pour the vinegar and apple cider into the pot and sprinkle with the brown sugar. Cover the pot, place in the oven, and braise for 3 hours, or until the pork is very tender.

Increase oven temperature to 400°F, remove the lid, and cook for another 30 minutes, or until the pork is golden brown. Remove from the oven and let it sit for 30 minutes for it to cool down and be easy enough to handle. Taste the sauce for seasoning, adding more salt and freshly ground black pepper if necessary. Remove the pork from the sauce and gently shred it. Add it back to the sauce and serve.

ROASTED FALL VEGETABLES WITH ITALIAN SAUSAGE

This recipe, if you can even call it that, is as family style as it gets. It is more of an idea than a recipe — one that comes in handy when you are exhausted but still want something hearty to eat and has the potential to feed lots of people as well.

I've used both uncooked and cooked sausages for this dish, and they both work. You can use vegetables you happen to have on hand or what is seasonal. I like to Greekify it a bit by sprinkling it with oregano and a squeeze of fresh lemon juice before roasting. I serve this sheet pan meal with a simple salad and fresh bread.

Serves 4 to 6

1 acorn squash, trimmed, cut in half lengthwise
Extra virgin olive oil
1½ pounds (680 g) white or red baby potatoes, cut in half
1 medium/large red onion, cut into 1-inch wedges
6 Italian sausages (sweet, hot, or a mix)
Juice of 1 lemon
Generous pinch of dried oregano
1 bunch kale, stemmed and torn into pieces (about 3 cups)
Salt and freshly ground black pepper
Extra virgin olive oil
1 handful flat-leaf parsley or cilantro, chopped, for garnish

Preheat the oven to 400°F (200°C) and line a sheet pan with parchment paper.

Cut the ends off the acorn squash and prop it up on your cutting board. Slice it down the middle lengthwise and remove the seeds. Cut the squash into 1-inch "smiles" by placing the flat part on your cutting board and cutting it horizontally. Toss with lots of olive oil, sprinkle with salt, and arrange over the baking sheet. Toss the baby potatoes with olive oil and add to the baking sheet with the squash.

Nestle the wedges of red onion randomly in between the squash where there is space (this keeps the onion wedges intact) and drizzle with a bit more olive oil.

Pierce the sausages a few times with a sharp knife and place on the baking sheet, in between the vegetables. Drizzle each sausage with a little olive oil.

Juice the lemon over the vegetables and sausages, then sprinkle the oregano over them.

Toss the kale with a bit of olive oil (so each piece is coated) and a sprinkle of salt and freshly ground black pepper and set aside.

Roast the vegetables and sausages in the oven for 30 to 40 minutes. Remove from the oven and place the kale on top of the baking sheet. Roast for another 10 minutes, or until everything is starting to crisp up and get golden brown. Drizzle with olive oil and garnish with parsley or cilantro and serve.

FRICASSEE
(BRAISED LAMB WITH ROMAINE, LEMON, AND DILL)

This is a popular springtime dish in Greece. The lamb is cooked until it is super tender and then covered in a thick *avgolemono*, a traditional egg and lemon sauce. Chopped romaine (often a cooked green in other countries) is added and cooked with a finishing touch of lots of fresh dill.

Serves 6 to 8

For the lamb:
Extra virgin olive oil
2½ pounds (1 kg) lamb shoulder, cut into 3-inch stew pieces
2 bunches scallions, white and light green parts only, chopped
1 bunch dill, chopped (about 1 cup / 60 g)
1 head romaine lettuce, cut into 1-inch pieces
Salt and freshly ground black pepper

For the *avgolemono*:
2 eggs
Juice of 2 lemons
Salt and freshly ground pepper

To make the lamb: heat a generous drizzle of olive oil in a heavy-bottomed pot over medium-high heat. Sprinkle the lamb liberally with salt and freshly ground black pepper and sear the chunks of lamb in batches, until golden brown.

Reduce the heat to medium-low and add the scallions and half of the dill. Return the lamb to the pot and add enough water to barely cover the lamb. Cover with a lid, increase the heat, and bring to a boil. Reduce the heat to low and simmer until the lamb is very tender, about 2½ to 3 hours. Add the lettuce to the lamb and cook until it is nice and soft, about 10 more minutes.

To make the *avgolemono*: in a medium bowl, whisk the eggs with the lemon juice and very slowly add a ladle of broth, whisking the whole time. Whisk in another two ladles of broth, then slowly drizzle the *avgolemono* back into the pot with the lamb, stirring the entire time.

Turn the heat back on to low and stir until it just starts to simmer. The broth should be velvety and thick like the consistency of heavy cream. Turn the heat off once again and taste for seasoning, adding salt and freshly ground black pepper as needed. Garnish with remaining dill and serve.

STEAK SEARED WITH FRIED FRESH OREGANO

A little while ago I had loads of beautiful, fresh, bright green oregano that I didn't know what to do with. I spent a week applying it to everything I was cooking; I tossed it with roasted vegetables and meats, I dried half of it, and I even thought about oregano ice cream (and decided against it).

On a whim, I pressed the sprigs into steaks that I seared on the stovetop. It looked beautiful, like when you press flowers in a book, and the searing imparted a lovely herby flavor to the meat. I also seared the rest of the whole oregano sprigs alongside the steak and ate them like aromatic salty potato chips. The squeeze of lemon at the end is the perfect finish, brightening up the whole dish.

Sage would also work well here, as it is another herb that crisps up nicely.

Serves 2 to 4

1½ pounds (680 g) bone-in rib eye steak
Kosher salt and freshly ground black pepper
1 bunch of fresh oregano sprigs
Extra virgin olive oil
1 lemon cut in half for serving

Heat a large, heavy skillet drizzled with a little olive oil over medium-high heat. Sprinkle the steak generously with salt and some grindings of freshly ground black pepper. Press three or four oregano sprigs onto one side of the steak (leaving the other side with only salt and pepper). Sear the steak for 5 minutes per side for medium-rare—start with pressed herb side first. When you flip the steak add the rest of the oregano sprigs to the pan during the last minute of cooking, allowing them to fry in the oil until crispy and brown. Remove the steak and oregano sprigs from the pan and let the steak rest for 10 minutes. Remove the herbs. Slice on the diagonal and serve with the fried herbs around the plate. Drizzle with a little bit of olive oil and a squeeze of lemon to serve.

CHICKEN BRAISED IN CINNAMON AND CUMIN WITH TAHINI

The warm and aromatic flavors of this dish envelop you in a cloud of comfort as they float through the house. It is a saucy chicken dish, simple yet full of flavor, with spices that are very Greek but also incorporate a visit to the Middle East. I like to serve this with whipped lemony tahini as a contrast to the sweet, spicy flavor of the tomato sauce. A side of buttery Basmati Rice with Cumin Seeds, Cinnamon, and Butter (page 132) is a perfect pairing.

Serves 4 to 6

For the chicken:
1 whole chicken, cut into 10 pieces (cut the breasts into 4 pieces; reserve the wings and backbone for another use)
1 large yellow onion, sliced into half-moons
1 head garlic
2 bay leaves
1 cinnamon stick
2 tablespoons ground cumin
1 (28-ounce / 794-g) can whole peeled tomatoes
2 teaspoons granulated sugar

Extra virgin olive oil
Salt and freshly ground black pepper
1 handful of flat-leaf parsley or cilantro, chopped, for garnish

For the tahini:
½ cup (120 ml) tahini
Juice of 1 lemon
¼ cup (60ml) water
Salt

Generously season the chicken pieces with salt and freshly ground black pepper.

Drizzle a bit of olive oil into a large pan and heat over medium-high heat. Add the chicken, skin-side down, and sear until golden brown, about 5 to 8 minutes. Remove from the pan and set aside. Reduce the heat to low and add the onions and a good drizzle of olive oil. Cook the onions for 1 minute, adding a splash (about ¼ cup) of water to scrape up the golden bits from the bottom of the pan. Slice off just the top of the head of garlic so the cloves are exposed. Remove most of the loose papers around the garlic. Add it whole to the pan with the onions, then add the bay leaves, cinnamon stick, and cumin.

Cook for 1 minute, then add the tomatoes and sugar. Add the chicken pieces, skin-side up, and just enough water so that just the top of the chicken pieces peek through the sauce. Bring to a simmer, then lower the heat, cover, and simmer for 60 minutes, until the sauce is thick and the chicken is very tender and soft. The sauce should have the consistency of heavy cream. If it is too thin, remove the lid for the last 10 minutes of cooking in order to thicken it. Allow to cool, taste, and add more salt and freshly ground black pepper if necessary.

To make the tahini: while the chicken is cooking, whisk together the tahini, lemon juice, water, and a pinch of salt until the sauce is thick and creamy.

I like to serve this dish with the tahini in a bowl alongside the chicken, or spread as thick layer on the bottom of a serving dish with the chicken spooned on top. Garnish with chopped parsley or cilantro and serve.

SOUTZOUKAKIA (CUMIN-SCENTED MEATBALLS WITH TOMATO SAUCE)

Soutzoukakia, easy-to-make meatballs, were a staple in my household growing up. As soon as I walked through the door from school, that warm familiar scent of my mother's cooking would surround and comfort me. A few *soutzoukakia* would be served on a plate with a perfect dome of white rice my mother would push into a teacup and unmold to my delight.

Alex and I have made *soutzoukakia* for many Christmas parties, serving the saucy meatballs with toothpicks and little plates to catch the sauce. The rich scent of cumin, garlic, and tomatoes simmering on the stove offers a warm welcome to the guests.

Serves 4

For the sauce:
4 tomatoes, grated, or 1 (8-ounce / 227-g) can tomato sauce
2 tablespoons extra virgin olive oil
1 teaspoon granulated sugar (optional)
Salt and freshly ground black pepper

For the meatballs:
1 pound (500 g) ground beef or turkey
1 small onion, grated on the large holes of a box grater, gently squeezed of juice
1 garlic clove, grated
1 tablespoon ground cumin
1½ teaspoons of kosher salt
Freshly ground black pepper
Extra virgin olive oil

To make the sauce: in a medium saucepan, if you're using grated tomatoes, combine them with the olive oil, the sugar (if using), and a pinch of salt and freshly ground black pepper. Bring to a simmer over medium-high heat, then reduce the heat and simmer for 20 to 25 minutes until it thickens up and the olive oil takes on a rich red color. If you're using tomato sauce, combine it with ½ cup (120 ml) water, the olive oil, a pinch of salt and freshly ground black pepper, and the sugar, if using, and simmer for 15 to 20 minutes. The olive oil floating in the sauce will have a golden red color and the sauce will be thick and deep red.

To make the meatballs: combine the ground beef, onion, garlic, cumin, kosher salt, and a few grindings of black pepper in a large bowl and briefly knead together until combined. Form the meat mixture into oval shapes about 3 inches long (makes 10 to 12 meatballs). Drizzle enough oil to coat the bottom of a large skillet and heat over medium-high heat. Add the meatballs and fry until golden brown, turning a few times. My mother says, "Just until they get some color." Add them to the tomato sauce and simmer until just cooked through, another 5 to 7 minutes.

BIFTEKIA (OVEN MEATBALLS WITH LEMON AND OREGANO)

The word "meatballs" is not a perfect translation here . . . *biftekia* are more of an oven burger without a bun, a meat patty. A better translation is a yummy, lemony, oven-baked delight that comes together very quickly, melts in your mouth, and delivers lots of flavor. Ground meat is simply seasoned with grated onion and oregano, then doused with lots of olive oil and lemon juice to create a liquid gold sauce the *biftekia* swim in when you take them out of the oven. For the perfect bite, make sure to dip a bite in the olive oil and lemon juice that's been simmering in the pan. Pair these with Tzatziki (page 30) to dip the potatoes in and a Georgian-Inspired Greek Salad with Herbs (page 57) for a real treat.

Serves 4

½ cup (120 ml) extra virgin olive oil, divided
1 slice sandwich bread or similar bread, soaked in water
  for 20 seconds and gently squeezed
1 pound (500 g) ground beef or turkey
2 teaspoons kosher salt, plus more as needed
1 teaspoon dried oregano, preferably Greek, plus more to sprinkle on top
1 small onion, grated on the large holes of a box grater and squeezed
  of excess moisture
3 to 4 russet or Yukon Gold potatoes, sliced into 8 wedges each
Juice of 2 lemons
Freshly ground black pepper

Preheat the oven to 400°F (200°C) and pour ¼ cup (60 ml) of the olive oil into the bottom of an 11 × 9–inch baking pan or a similar-size large round baking pan.

Remove the crust from the bread and tear it into very small pieces with your hands, as small as you can get them. In a large bowl, mix the ground meat with the salt, a generous pinch of dried oregano, grated onion, and bread.

To form the *biftekia*, wet your hands, take about ⅓ cup (60g) cup of the meat mixture, and form it into a ball, slightly pressing down on top to flatten it to about a 4-inch plump oval. Repeat with the rest of the meat.

You should end up with 7 or 8 *biftekia*. Place the *biftekia* in the oiled pan, slightly spaced apart.

Rinse the potato wedges in cold water, then place them in a bowl and toss with ¼ cup (60 ml) olive oil and a large pinch of salt. Place between and around the *biftekia* in the pan.

Squeeze the lemons over the potatoes and *biftekia*. Sprinkle with a little more salt, oregano, and lots of freshly ground black pepper.

Roast in the oven for 45 to 50 minutes. This is a soft dish, not one with lots of golden-brown caramelization.

BEANS AND LENTILS

During the summer on the Greek island of Paros, there's something called the Chickpea Festival in the historic village of Prodromos. People from all over the island gather to honor the amazing chickpea, once cultivated on the Cycladic Islands, and now celebrated annually by being cooked in the last remaining wood-burning oven on the island.

The chickpeas are soaked and then placed on large baking trays with onions and lots of local olive oil. Then they're transferred to the wood-burning oven and slow-cooked overnight. The women of the village pull out hot trays and scoop out plump chickpeas soaked in olive oil for hungry locals and tourists to sample.

That's all it takes to make one of the world's most nutritious foods taste delicious—a handful of ingredients and a hands-off approach to cooking them. I apply this technique to making beans and lentils in all kinds of ways—whether it's in the oven or on the stovetop.

If I'm using beans in a stew or cooking them in the oven, I most often use dried beans that have been soaked; soaked beans create a delicious sauce or broth in the respective dish and add a lot of flavor.

When it comes to soaking beans, I use a few different methods. I most often soak the beans anywhere from 8 to 16 hours. I use a big bowl for 1 pound of dried beans, and I fill it almost to the top with cold water. I cover it with a towel or a lid and set it a cool spot. In the morning, I either drain and cook them immediately, or drain, place in an airtight container, and stick them in the refrigerator until I am ready to use them (up to two days). In the summertime, I often place the bowl of soaking beans in the refrigerator because the heat can cause the beans to start to ferment.

I rarely soak black beans because I love the deep purple color they impart, and I never soak black-eyed peas or lentils. If I'm making a cold bean salad, I use canned beans, which are convenient and just as good in this application.

My first job cooking at PS1 involved making food for Warm Up, a music festival held every summer in the courtyard of the museum, celebrating emerging and established musical acts and DJs. When we had to figure out how to cook for a crowd of five thousand people, I thought of that chickpea festival in Paros. Our menu for Warm Up consisted of Santorini Dogs (page 87) Cucumber Salad with Toasted Sesame Seeds, Dill and Parsley (page 54), and *Revithia sto Fourno* or Oven Chickpeas (page 110). The only difference in our version was that we served the chickpeas cold—after chilling them overnight—and with lots of lemon juice, more like a salad. They were a hit, refreshing yet filling in the summer heat, and relatively straightforward to prepare for the massive crowd.

I grew up eating bean and lentil dishes often as the main course with a side of olives, feta, and bread. I have retained this ethos when cooking for large events—it's important to learn how to "cook for the village." This type of cooking is usually unfussy, practical, and fine-tuned over the centuries to maximize flavor.

REVITHIA STO FOURNO
(OVEN CHICKPEAS)

This is the recipe I make the most in my house. It is our favorite comfort food.

I started making this staple dish after sampling the traditional recipe made (for centuries) by the women of Prodromos—truly a religious experience. Although the chickpeas appeared simple, the preparation was meticulous, and the taste was exceptional. Soaking the chickpeas overnight and cooking them for hours are the keys to unlocking their complex flavor and creating a rich texture. The slower cooking process allows the oven to do the work, giving the chickpeas plenty of time to absorb the flavor of the onions, garlic, and bay leaves. Cook the chickpeas with just a drizzle of olive oil and then add a whole lot more when they come out of the oven. If you want to serve them PS1 Warm Up–style, chill the chickpeas overnight and toss with chopped fresh parsley and more olive oil when you are ready to serve. It's the perfect dish for a hot summer evening.

This is a great main dish served with some olives, cheese, and bread.

Serves 8 to 10

1 pound (450 g) dried chickpeas, soaked (see page 108) and drained
2 medium yellow onions, sliced into quarters
6 to 8 whole garlic cloves (unpeeled)
4 bay leaves
Extra virgin olive oil
Juice of 2 lemons
Salt and freshly ground black pepper

Preheat the oven to 350°F (180°C).

Place the soaked chickpeas in an ovenproof casserole dish with a lid. Add fresh cold water to cover the chickpeas by 1 inch. Add the onions, garlic, bay leaves, a generous pinch of salt, and a drizzle of olive oil.

Bake for 4 hours, or until the chickpeas are very soft. Add the lemon juice and another drizzle of olive oil. Taste for seasoning and add more salt if necessary. Finish with freshly ground black pepper.

CHICKPEA SALAD WITH FETA AND HERBS

I love a chickpea salad. I make this salad for lunch regularly, and the leftovers keep very well for a few days. It's also just as lovely paired with a green salad for a summertime dinner.

You can substitute canned chickpeas with good results, but what's nice about cooking them yourself is that the chickpeas will absorb the olive oil and lemon juice better, making the salad extra tasty.

Another nice variation is to zest the lemons before squeezing them and add the zest to the salad as well. You can use any herbs you like, but parsley and dill hold up to the dressing. This recipe is easily halved if you want to make less.

Serves 6 to 8

1 pound (450 g) chickpeas, soaked (see page 108) and drained,
    or 2 (15-ounce / 425-g) cans of chickpeas, rinsed and drained
¾ cup (180 ml) extra virgin olive oil
Juice of 3 to 4 lemons
1 garlic clove, finely grated (optional)
1 pound (450 g) Greek feta, crumbled
3 cups (180 g) mixed green herbs, such as parsley,
    dill, and mint, chopped
A few mint leaves for garnish
Salt and freshly ground black pepper

Place the chickpeas in a large pot of salted water, bring to a simmer, and simmer until they are very soft, 1 to 1½ hours. Alternately, use the canned chickpeas.

Place the chickpeas in a large bowl. Whisk together the olive oil, lemon juice, and grated garlic clove, if using. Pour the dressing over the warm chickpeas and sprinkle the salad generously with salt. Toss to combine all the ingredients and set aside to cool in the refrigerator.

Once the salad has cooled down, taste for seasoning and add more salt if necessary (I find once the salad has chilled it needs another dose of seasoning), and gently toss in the crumbled feta and herbs. To serve, garnish with mint leaves, drizzle with olive oil, and crack lots of freshly ground black pepper on top.

BRAISED CHICKPEAS WITH ORANGE ZEST AND GARLIC BREADCRUMBS

I sat down for lunch one day at a restaurant in Athens called Nikitas and had a divine dish of chickpeas that was different from anything I had ever tasted. They were baked in the oven with lots of orange zest, something I would never have thought to add—and the results were amazing. My version of this dish adds crunchy olive oil–soaked breadcrumbs with orange zest and garlic for extra texture and flavor. The best bites are when some of the breadcrumbs soak in the lemony broth of the chickpeas and they absorb that flavor yet stay a bit crunchy.

Serves 8 to 10

For the chickpeas:
1 pound (450 g) dried chickpeas,
  soaked (see page 108) and drained
2 medium yellow onions, sliced into thin half-moons
2 bay leaves
Peel of 1 orange
Salt
Extra virgin olive oil
Juice of 2 lemons

For the breadcrumbs: (makes about 2 cups)
1 white baguette, day-old or fresh, ends discarded
  and torn into pieces
2 garlic cloves, peeled and left whole
About ⅓ cup (80 ml) extra virgin olive oil
Zest of 1 orange
Salt and freshly ground black pepper

To make the chickpeas: preheat the oven to 350°F (180°C).

Place the soaked chickpeas in an ovenproof casserole dish and add water to cover the chickpeas by 2 inches. Layer the onions, bay leaves, and orange peel on top, followed by a generous pinch of salt and a generous drizzle of olive oil. Cover with a lid.

Bake for 2½ to 3 hours, until the chickpeas are very soft. Add the lemon juice and another drizzle of olive oil. Taste for seasoning and add more salt if necessary.

To make the breadcrumbs: While the chickpeas are baking, place the torn bread in a food processor with the garlic cloves and pulse to the size of crumbs. Place in a bowl and add just enough olive oil to saturate the breadcrumbs, a good pinch of salt, and lots of freshly

ground black pepper. Spread on a baking sheet and toast, mixing once, until the breadcrumbs are golden brown, about 10 to 15 minutes. Remove from the oven and allow the breadcrumbs to cool down. Add the orange zest and toss to combine.

Top the chickpeas with about 1 cup (60 g) of the breadcrumbs (I usually serve this dish warm, in the vessel I cooked it in). Reserve the extra breadcrumbs for another use. I like to sprinkle them on a salad or pasta the next day.

FASOLADA (TRADITIONAL GREEK WHITE BEAN STEW)

The national dish of Greece is this simple, healthy, vegan bean stew with roots that date back to ancient Greece as a soup that was offered to the god Apollo.

I love to make this stew in the fall when the weather is just starting to chill. It's creamy and inviting, so simple, and pairs perfectly with some olives and bread. Be very generous with drizzling high-quality olive oil on top of the stew. It makes all the difference.

Serves 6 to 8

1 pound (450 g) navy or cannellini beans, soaked (see page 108)
  and drained
3 bay leaves
2 medium yellow onions, peeled
1 whole head garlic, washed, top cut off
1 (14½-ounce / 411-g) can whole peeled tomatoes
  (or 3 large fresh tomatoes, cut in half)
4 celery stalks, cut into ½-inch pieces
4 carrots, cut into ½-inch pieces
2 handfuls of flat-leaf parsley, chopped, for garnish
½ cup (120 ml) extra virgin olive oil, plus more for serving
Red chile flakes (optional)
Salt and freshly ground black pepper

Place the soaked beans in a large pot and cover them with 2 inches of cold water. Add the bay leaves, whole onions, and whole head of garlic. (Note: I like to wash the head of garlic well and cut off or remove as many of the roots and extra papery leaves as possible. I cut the top off to expose the garlic cloves while cooking.)

Add the tomatoes (they will break up as they cook). Add 2 large pinches of salt and bring the soup to a boil. Cover with the lid slightly ajar. Reduce the heat to medium-low, add the celery, and cook for 30 minutes. Add the carrots and cook for another 30 minutes, or until the beans are very soft. Turn off the heat and stir in the olive oil. Taste for seasoning and add more salt if necessary. Remove the whole onions, any tomato skins, and head of garlic.

Ladle the stew into bowls and top with a sprinkle of parsley and a drizzle of olive oil. Serve with red chile flakes, if using, and freshly ground black pepper on top.

BLACK BEAN STEW TOPPED WITH FETA, CILANTRO, AND JALAPEÑOS

A generous amount of cumin and lime juice infuse this otherwise basic dish with bright flavor. I usually don't soak the beans before making it because I like the deep purple color they add to the dish, but if you want to decrease the cooking time of the stew, you can soak your beans the night before.

The topping variations for this dish are endless, but I always love the combination of creamy salty feta, bright cilantro, and spicy jalapeños on top. Leftovers are great for black bean tacos, as the stew thickens up a bit after being refrigerated and is perfect for filling toasted corn tortillas.

Serves 8 to 10

1 pound (450 g) dried black beans
   (soaked, see page 108, and drained; optional)
1 large red or yellow onion, diced
4 bay leaves
¼ cup (30 g) ground cumin
¼ (60 ml) cup extra virgin olive oil
Juice of 2 limes
Salt and freshly ground black pepper

Toppings:
Crumbled feta
Fresh cilantro leaves
Thinly sliced jalapeño

Combine the beans, onion, bay leaves, and cumin in a large pot. Fill with water to cover the beans by 3 inches. Bring to a boil over high heat, then reduce the heat to medium-low and cook for 1½ to 2½ hours, adding a bit of water as needed to keep the beans covered by 1 inch. When the beans are very soft, remove from the heat and add 2 large pinches of salt, lots of freshly ground black pepper, the olive oil, and lime juice.

I adle the stew into serving bowls and top with feta, cilantro, and jalapeño rounds.

GIGANTES PLAKI

These traditional Greek-style beans I grew up on are baked in the oven for a long time, until they are very soft and the tomato and olive oil sauce have permeated every bean. *Plaki* means "spread out" or "flat" in Greek, and applies to this bean dish as the cooking vessel should be large enough so that the beans are generally cooked in a single layer. At the end they get blasted with high heat, which crisps them to a golden brown. Serve as a main dish with wedges of feta and a simple cucumber salad.

Serves 6 to 8

1 pound (450 g) gigante beans, soaked overnight (see page 108)
  and drained
1 large red onion, cut into 8 wedges
8 garlic cloves, peeled and left whole
1 (28-ounce / 794-g) can whole or pureed tomatoes
Extra virgin olive oil
Salt and freshly ground black pepper

Preheat the oven to 350°F (180°C).

In a Dutch oven with a lid (or another ovenproof pan with lid, or make a lid out of aluminum foil), combine the beans, onion, garlic, and tomatoes. Add enough water so the liquid hovers over the beans by 2 inches and mix to combine the ingredients. Drizzle generously with olive oil and sprinkle with salt and freshly ground black pepper.

Cover and cook in the oven for 3 hours, or until the beans are very soft and the liquid is saucy. Add a little water if it needs to loosen up a bit. Increase the oven temperature to 425°F (220°C) and continue to cook uncovered until the beans get a little golden color on top. Drizzle with more olive oil and serve.

BLACK-EYED PEAS WITH CELERY, LEMON, AND PARSLEY

Black-eyed pea salad, or *mavromatika*, is a staple on the lunchtime table in Greece that consists of black-eyed peas, chopped tomatoes, parsley, and red wine vinegar. My spin on the classic salad is fresh, crunchy, and bright green, something I started to make in the winter when tomatoes aren't in season. I generally prefer using lemon juice in place of vinegar—it has a lighter, cleaner flavor—and I enjoy the different shades of green from the celery and parsley. One thing I have learned when dressing beans is that it is important to dress the salad and then taste it again after it has soaked in the dressing for an hour or so. I often find the black-eyed peas need another drizzle, squeeze, and sprinkle of everything to really pop with flavor. This dish is a beautiful side to Arctic Char with Crispy Cumin Crust (page 66) and can stand alone as a vegetarian main dish served with a green salad, such as Baby Lettuces with Toasted Sesame Seeds, Mint, and Meyer Lemon Yogurt (page 40).

Serves 6 to 8

1 pound (450 g) dried black-eyed peas
6 celery stalks, finely chopped
1 bunch flat-leaf or curly parsley, finely chopped
4 scallions, white and light green parts, thinly sliced (optional)
Juice of 2 to 4 lemons
½ cup (120 ml) extra virgin olive oil
Salt and freshly ground black pepper

Bring a large pot of salted water to a boil. Add the black-eyed peas, lower the heat to medium, and cover with the lid slightly ajar. Cook until the beans are very tender and creamy in the middle, 1 to 1½ hours. They will firm up a bit as they cool. Drain in a colander, then transfer to a large bowl. Toss the black-eyed peas with the celery, parsley, scallions, lemon juice, and olive oil. Season with salt and freshly ground black pepper and serve.

FRENCH LENTILS WITH CARAMELIZED FENNEL AND GOLDEN RAISINS

Little compares to this delightful combination of fennel, golden raisins, and olive oil–soaked French lentils. Instead of sauteing the fennel, sometimes I'll roast it in the oven to get an even deeper caramel color. The savory flavor is balanced by sweet pops of golden raisins and herby freshness of the parsley. It is an inviting platform for additions such as a variety of green herbs or crumbled feta, yet also perfect on its own.

Serves 6 to 8

2 cups (420 g) dried French lentils
2 bay leaves
1 large red onion, sliced into thin half-moons
1 fennel bulb, cored and sliced into thin half-moons
¾ cup (110 g) golden raisins
Extra virgin olive oil
Salt and freshly ground black pepper
2 handfuls flat-leaf parsley, finely chopped

Bring a large pot of salted water to a boil and add the lentils and bay leaves. Reduce the heat to medium-low and simmer until the lentils are tender, about 20 minutes. Drain the lentils, remove the bay leaves, and return the lentils to the pot. Drizzle with a little olive oil and set aside.

Drizzle a generous amount of olive oil into a large skillet over medium heat. Add the onion, fennel, and a large pinch of salt and freshly ground black pepper. Cook until the onion and fennel get some golden color, then add the raisins and cook for a few minutes more, turning up the heat to get a golden color on the onion and fennel if necessary. Add the lentils and mix gently to incorporate.

Alternatively, preheat the oven to 400°F. Line a baking sheet with parchment paper. Place the fennel and onion on a baking sheet in an even layer (it's OK to mix them). Drizzle generously with olive oil and sprinkle with salt and freshly ground pepper. Roast until golden brown, about 30 minutes, adding the raisins during the last 3 minutes of roasting. Remove the fennel mixture from the oven, add the lentils directly to the roasting pan, and toss to incorporate all the ingredients.

Right before serving, gently toss in the parsley, reserving some to sprinkle on top.

OVEN-BRAISED LENTILS

I went through a period of time when I completely abandoned stovetop cooking. I made everything in the oven because it meant I had to do next to nothing, with excellent results. I took a stovetop Greek lentil stew called *faki* and cooked it in the oven instead, and sometimes added seasonal vegetables I had on hand (sweet potatoes, carrots, and butternut squash work really well). The result was a warming main casserole-style dish you can serve with plain Greek yogurt and a salad.

Serves 6 to 8

1 pound (450 g) brown lentils
1 medium/large yellow onion, diced
2 whole heads garlic, with the tops sliced off
2 bay leaves
1 (28-ounce / 794-g) can tomato puree
2 medium sweet potatoes or 4 large carrots,
　peeled and cut into bite-size pieces (optional)
4 cups (945 ml) water
Extra virgin olive oil
Salt and freshly ground black pepper
Red wine vinegar for serving (optional)
Red chile flakes for serving (optional)

Preheat the oven to 350°F (180°C).

Combine the lentils, onion, garlic, bay leaves, tomato puree, and sweet potatoes, if using, in an oven-safe baking dish with a lid. Add the water and a generous splash of olive oil and season with salt and freshly ground black pepper. Bake for 1½ hours, or until most of the liquid has been absorbed and the lentils are nice and soft. Check seasoning, adding more salt and freshly ground black pepper to taste. To serve, drizzle with olive oil and (if using) a splash of vinegar and a sprinkle of red chile flakes.

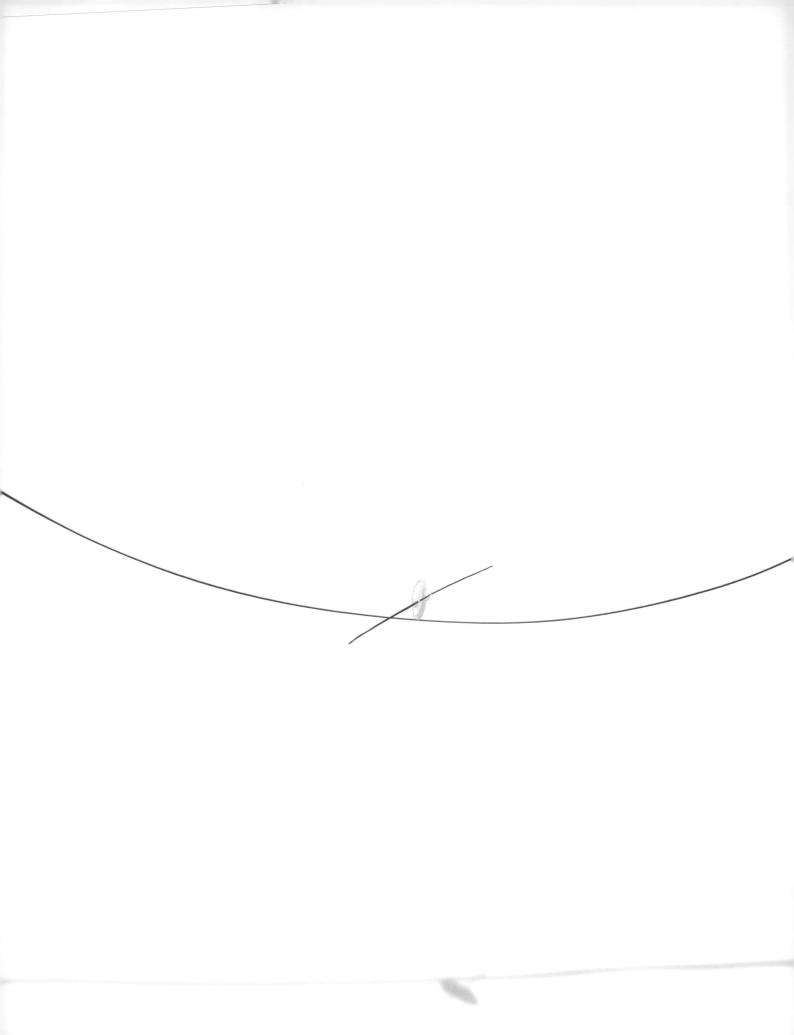

RICE

My mother and I call each other often. My favorite time to talk to her is when I'm driving, stuck in NYC traffic and alone in the car. She's on speaker, full blast. She wishes I'd call her even more than I already do, but I guess that's a mother-daughter dynamic most women can relate to.

During one of my favorite recent phone calls, we talked about rice, and she mentioned that her standout memory of rice was something called *lapa*, a traditional Greek way of cooking rice when someone is sick.

Lapa translates to "mushy," and consists of short-grain rice cooked in chicken broth or water until it is very, very soft and falling apart. Then, lots of lemon juice is mixed in and it's served as a soothing and healing antidote usually for stomach upset or fever.

The rice dish that my mother remembers as a child is very different from mine. I remember often asking her to make me *soutzoukakia*, cumin and garlic–scented meatballs swimming in tomato sauce (recipe, page 103). I loved when she made this dish for me because alongside it came a special treat: a beautiful, perfect dome of rice. It was all I saw on the plate as a child.

My mom would press the rice into a teacup and then unmold it on my plate. She would spoon the meatballs and sauce on the side, and I ate it with pure joy and reverence, amazed she could perform such magic.

The charm in that dome of rice has more history to it than I once thought. I imagined it only as my mother's clever invention, but rice, until recent history, was a food of luxury in Greece. You'll find that lingering awe in the way it is used today. Rice was often served in a molded shape throughout Greece and the Middle East to designate it as a very special food—hence how my mother served it, molded in a teacup, like my grandmother taught her.

Rice still suggests celebration and opulence on special occasions in Greece. In everyday life, rice has been integrated to enrich a variety of traditional recipes. It holds that spiritual duality as a part of its identity—something that can be very special, yet also everyday and comforting. Pretty similar to the phone calls I have with my mom.

BASMATI RICE WITH CUMIN SEEDS, CINNAMON, AND BUTTER

This is a lovely and simple aromatic rice that fills your home with the warming spices of cumin and cinnamon. I make this dish when I want something that will pair beautifully with a saucy meat dish, such as Chicken Braised in Cinnamon and Cumin with Tahini (page 100). There are few things better than mouthfuls of fragrant rice that has absorbed lots of delicious sauce.

Serves 6 to 8

2 cups (400 g) basmati rice
3 cups (750 ml) water
2 bay leaves
1 tablespoon cumin seeds
1 whole cinnamon stick
4 tablespoons (60 g) butter
Salt

Rinse the rice four or five times in cold water, until it runs mostly clear. Place it in a medium to large pot and add the water, bay leaves, cumin seeds, cinnamon stick, butter, and a good pinch of salt. Bring to boil, then reduce the heat to low and cover. Cook until the water is absorbed and the rice is tender, about 12 minutes. Remove from heat. Remove the lid and cover with a kitchen towel. The towel absorbs the steam so it doesn't drip back onto the rice. Allow the rice to rest for 10 minutes before fluffing and serving.

RED RICE SALAD WITH GREEN HERBS, CURRANTS, AND FETA

I like using red, brown, or black rice in this salad. They are all varieties that hold up well to the olive oil and lemon juice dressing and are hearty grains that have a little crunch to them. This is a dish that lends itself to versatility; you can swap the currants for other dried fruits, such as chopped apricots, dried cherries, or golden raisins. Adding toasted nuts and seeds is also delicious.

Serves 6 to 8

2 cups (400 g) red rice (brown and black rice
  are good substitutes)
1 tablespoon (15 g) butter
1 cup (20 g) herbs, such as parsley, cilantro,
  and mint, coarsely chopped
½ cup (75 g) currants
Juice of 2 lemons
⅓ cup (80 ml) extra virgin olive oil
Salt and freshly ground black pepper
¾ cup (150 g) crumbled feta

Bring a large pot of salted water to a rolling boil. Add the rice and cook until it is nice and tender, 40 to 45 minutes (this cooking process is similar to cooking pasta). Drain the rice in a colander and add the butter.

Place the rice in a large bowl and allow it to cool down, fluffing it occasionally. Add the herbs and currants and gently toss. Add the lemon juice and olive oil and season with salt and freshly ground black pepper. Toss again until just combined. Add the feta and gently mix it in to serve.

UZBEK-STYLE RICE WITH LAMB, TOASTED ALMONDS, GOLDEN RAISINS, AND APRICOTS

This is my take on the national dish of Uzbekistan. *Plov*, or pilaf, is made in a huge *kazan*, or cast-iron wok with lots of oil, rice, dried fruits and nuts, and meat—often lamb. *Plov* is a main dish served both at celebrations and everyday occasions. Every mouthful pops with flavors that are sweet, salty, fresh, and robust, with a variety of textures to delight the mouth. I would order a plate of it as often as possible at a traditional Uzbek food stand in Moscow while I was cooking for Urs Fischer's exhibition at the Garage Museum of Contemporary Art. You can do a different meat or fruit and nut combination depending on what you like.

Serves 4 to 6

2 tablespoons (30 g) butter
Extra virgin olive oil
1 large onion, diced
1 pound (450 g) boneless leg of lamb,
  cut into bite-size pieces
1 tablespoon ground cumin
4 carrots, grated on the large holes of a box grater
½ cup (150 g) golden raisins

½ cup (150 g) dried apricots, sliced into slivers
1½ cups (300 g) basmati rice, rinsed four or
  five times, until the water runs clear
2 bay leaves
1 cup (145 g) almonds, toasted (see page 9)
  and chopped
Salt and freshly ground black pepper
2 handfuls of flat-leaf parsley, chopped, for garnish

Set a tea kettle with 3 cups (750 ml) water to boil. In a large pot or heavy pan with a lid, melt the butter in a drizzle of olive oil over low heat. Add the onion and a good pinch of salt and cook until the onion starts to soften, about 3 minutes.

Season the lamb with salt and freshly ground black pepper. Turn the heat to medium-high and add the lamb. Don't move the pieces around too much; let them get some golden-brown color on at least one side. Add the cumin, stir to combine, and cook for another minute.

Remove the onion and lamb from the pan and set aside. Add a little more olive oil to the pan, add the carrots, and cook for 1 minute. Add the raisins and apricots and cook for another minute. Return the lamb and onion mixture to the pan and toss to combine.

Add the rice, reduce the heat to medium, and cook for 3 minutes. Add the boiling water and bay leaves and reduce the heat to low. Cover and cook for 18 to 20 minutes until the rice is cooked through. Allow to rest for 10 minutes, then fluff, toss in the toasted almonds, and garnish with the parsley.

RICE AND STARS PILAF

Toasted, golden-brown buttery pasta folded into fluffy rice? Yes please, any day, I'll take it.

I have had many variations over the years—some from the hands of Cypriot and Turkish friends, and others at Middle Eastern restaurants. The one I love to make the most (kid pleaser alert) is with small star-shaped pasta that feels sophisticated yet pretty and maybe even a little magical. You can substitute orzo for the star pasta.

Serves 6 to 8

1 cup (200 g) long-grain rice, such as basmati or jasmine
2 tablespoons (30 g) butter
2 tablespoons extra virgin olive oil
1 cup (190 g) small star-shaped pasta
Salt

Soak the rice in cold water for 20 minutes, then drain and rinse four or five times, until the water runs clear.

In a large pot, melt the butter in the olive oil over medium-low heat. Add the star pasta and a large pinch of salt and cook until the pasta is light golden brown, about 4 minutes. Add the rice and cook for 1 minute longer, stirring to combine. Add 2½ cups (590 ml) hot water and another large pinch of salt and reduce the heat to low. Cover the pot and cook for 12 to 15 minutes, until the rice is tender and the water is absorbed. Remove the lid and let stand, covered with a dish towel, for 10 minutes. Fluff the pilaf and serve.

CYPRIOT BULGUR WITH TOASTED PASTA AND TOMATO

Some of the best food I have ever had was on a thirty six-hour trip I made to Cyprus to visit my friend Phillipos. His mother, seemingly with no effort at all, made us Cypriot delights, rolled out elegantly at their kitchen table. One of the things I enjoyed most was this comforting pilaf she served alongside Cypriot sausage and fried Halloumi cheese.

Serves 6

2 tablespoons (30 g) butter
2 tablespoons extra virgin olive oil
1 small yellow onion, finely chopped
½ cup (100 g) angel hair pasta, broken into small pieces
1 cup (150 g) bulgur wheat
¾ cup (180 ml) tomato puree
2 cups (480 ml) water or broth
Salt and freshly ground black pepper

Melt the butter in the olive oil in a medium heavy-bottomed pot over low heat. Add the onion and a good pinch of salt and freshly ground black pepper. Cook until the onion starts to soften, about 3 minutes. Turn the heat up to medium and add the broken angel hair pasta. Cook until the pasta is golden brown.

Add the bulgur wheat and sauté briefly until all the ingredients are incorporated with the bulgur. Add the tomato puree and water or broth and bring to a boil over high heat. Reduce the heat to low, cover with a lid slightly ajar, and simmer until all the liquid is absorbed, 5 to 8 minutes. Remove from the heat and drape a kitchen towel over the pot to absorb the steam. Allow to sit for 10 minutes, then fluff with a fork and serve.

GREEN RICE

In this dish fresh herbs impart a color and flavor that quickly brightens and elevates an otherwise simple rice preparation. Many recipes for green rice call for cooking the herbs along with the rice and the water, but I prefer to cook the rice and then mix in the herbs at the end, so the dish stays bright green and very fresh. Sometimes I add toasted pine nuts for an extra pop of deliciousness.

Serves 4 to 6

1½ cups (300 g) basmati or jasmine rice
2⅔ cups (720 ml) water
1 small yellow onion, chopped
2 tablespoons (30 g) butter
2 bay leaves
1 cup (20 g) parsley leaves
1 cup (20 g) cilantro leaves
1 cup (20 g) mint leaves
Salt and freshly ground black pepper
½ cup (90 g) pine nuts, toasted (see page 9; optional)

Rinse the rice four or five times, until the water runs clear. If you have extra time, generously salt a large bowl of water and let the rice soak for 15 minutes. Drain.

Place the drained rice in a pot with the 2⅔ cups (700 ml) water, the onion, butter, bay leaves, and a good pinch of salt. Bring to a boil over high heat. Stir the rice once, then reduce the heat to low and cover. Cook until the rice is fully cooked, 15 to 20 minutes. If it is not done, add ¼ cup (60 ml) more water and continue to cook the rice over low heat. Let the rice sit, covered with a kitchen towel, for 10 minutes, then fluff with a fork.

In a food processor fitted with the blade attachment, pulse the herbs until they are finely chopped, almost as fine as a paste. Fold the herbs in gently to the rice until fully incorporated and bright green. Alternatively, chop the herbs as finely as you can with a sharp knife. Fold in the toasted pine nuts, if using, add some freshly ground black pepper, and serve.

PASTA

I have a romantic view of pasta.

My daydream involves spaghetti. Twirling it around on my fork paired with lots of red wine in a wineglass that's obscenely large. I'm channeling some of the beautiful Italian women I've seen do the same thing, so naturally, as if pasta is nothing . . . a cool breeze that doesn't touch down on the body in any way.

It's a chilly night in New York City, and I picture all of us around the table dishing up lots of pasta to our friends. I make two whole boxes for four people because that's how much pasta we like to eat. I've always related to the book *Strega Nona*, where there's unlimited pasta boiling out of the witch's pot and there's no anxiety or preciousness in terms of how much pasta is available to eat.

Pasta embodies a fantasy. It is my ideal dinner table of happiness. It's the opposite of loneliness. I transport myself back to my childhood, post-beach, plain spaghetti, smothered with Fytini, the Greek version of terrible-for-you hydrogenated margarine that makes everything taste great. Covered in a cloud of *kefalograviera*—a hard, salty, and delicious Greek cheese—I am in paradise. A sleepy, fluffy, Mediterranean dream.

In reality, at our house, pasta is made on the fly and kept very simple. As much as I love to have ample time to cook, sometimes it's far from possible. Some of the best things I've cooked were made out of necessity, and my pasta recipes often reflect this approach. It's a combination of unpretentious cupboard ingredients or leftovers or an untraditional pesto. It comes together quickly, flavors commingling in pleasure, spaghetti twirling to the max, always in abundance, and hopefully with friends.

PASTA WITH TOASTED ALMOND AND LEMON PESTO

This simple spaghetti dish is made with an untraditional pesto that has the bold flavors of citrus and toasty almonds. It's light and vegan, and I usually make it with brown rice pasta, making it gluten free as well. The lemony toasted almond and lemon pesto is a home run, wrapping everything up in a warm, delicious hug.

Serves 4

½ cup (70 g) almonds, toasted (see page 9)
Zest of 2 lemons
Juice of 3 lemons (about ⅓ cup / 80 ml)
⅓ cup (80 ml) extra virgin olive oil
⅓ cup (80 ml) water
1 pound (500 g) spaghetti or pasta of your choice
Salt and freshly ground black pepper

To make the almond and lemon pesto, in a food processor or high-powered blender, combine the almonds, lemon zest, lemon juice, olive oil, and water. Process or blend on high speed until the mixture is thick and creamy. If it is too thick, add a little more water and blend again.

Bring a large pot of salted water to a boil, add the pasta, and cook until al dente. Drain and toss with the pesto and taste for seasoning, adding more salt if necessary. Finish with lots of freshly ground black pepper and serve.

EGG NOODLES WITH GRATED TOMATOES AND LEMON ZEST

We make this pasta twice a week in August, when the tomatoes are juicy and bountiful, and the summertime heat allows for minimal cooking. This pasta is Alex's invention—with just a few seasonal ingredients and special techniques (like soaking a whole garlic clove in the grated tomato!), he transforms egg noodles into a flavorful and light dish.

Serves 4

4 large tomatoes
Zest of 2 lemons
2 garlic cloves, peeled and left whole
¼ cup (60 ml) extra virgin olive oil
1 pound (500 g) egg noodles or linguini
½ pound (250 g) Greek hard cheese for grating, such as
   kefalotyri or *kefalograviera* (Parmesan is a great substitute)
Salt and freshly ground black pepper

Grate the tomatoes on the large holes of a box grater and discard the peel. Pass the grated tomato through a fine-mesh strainer so you are just left with the pulp. Place the pulp in a bowl and add the lemon zest and garlic. (Alex lets the garlic cloves soak in the tomato mixture and removes them before tossing in the pasta.) Whisk in the olive oil and a big pinch of salt

Bring a large pot of salted water to a boil, add the pasta, and cook until al dente. Drain the pasta, transfer to a serving bowl, and toss with the tomato sauce. Discard the garlic cloves. Grate the cheese, toss most of it with the pasta, and use the rest to garnish the top. Add freshly ground black pepper over the pasta and serve.

ONE-POT SPAGHETTI WITH TOMATOES, CAPERS, AND BASIL

Initially, the idea of one-pot spaghetti really tickled my fancy for the least number of dishes dirtied during dinner prep. I thought it might be impossible, but I tried anyway, skeptical but optimistic.

As I discovered, it's not only possible to cook pasta as a one-pot meal; it's awesome—it makes an al dente pasta, swimming in its own velvety sauce. The tricks are to break the pasta in half and *just* cover the pasta in boiling water. Both facilitate adding just the right amount of water so the pasta ends up perfectly cooked.

This simple combination of sweet tomatoes, salty capers, and fragrant basil covered with good olive oil is summertime in a bowl.

Serves 4

4 garlic cloves, chopped
1 pound (500 g) spaghetti, broken in half
1 pint (300 g) cherry tomatoes, halved
¼ cup (65 g) salt-packed capers, rinsed well
Extra virgin olive oil
Red chile flakes (optional)
1 cup (20 g) loosely torn basil, for garnish
Salt and freshly ground black pepper

Heat a teapot filled with water until boiling. This will be your pasta water.

Pour a generous drizzle of olive oil into a large pot. Add the garlic and a large pinch of salt. Cook over low heat for a 3 minutes, until fragrant but not browned.
Add the pasta to the garlic and olive oil, then add enough hot water just to cover the pasta by ½ inch. Turn the heat up to high and bring to a rolling boil. Add the cherry tomatoes to the pot and gently distribute them with tongs.

Cook uncovered over medium-high heat until the pasta is al dente. Remove from the heat. Sprinkle the pasta with the capers and drizzle with lots of olive oil. Finish with red chile flakes and the torn basil and season with salt and freshly ground black pepper.

PAPPARDELLE WITH CHICKPEAS, LEMON, AND TOASTED WALNUTS

One night I had a batch of leftover Oven Chickpeas (page 110) and some beautiful handmade pappardelle noodles. Knowing the Italians have a chickpea and pasta dish called *pasta e ceci*, I thought I'd give it a try—and this is the result. Of course, I've Greekified it with the addition of lots of lemon juice and a topping of freshly toasted walnuts.

Serves 4

1 pound (500 g) pappardelle
2 tablespoons (30 g) butter
2 garlic cloves, finely grated
1 (15-ounce / 425-g) can chickpeas, rinsed and drained,
   or 1¾ cups leftover Oven Chickpeas (page 110)
Zest and juice of 2 lemons
Extra virgin olive oil
Salt and freshly ground black pepper
½ cup (60 g) walnuts, toasted with olive oil and salt (see page 9)
   and finely chopped

Bring a large pot of salted water to a boil, add the pasta, and cook until al dente. Drain, drizzle with a bit of olive oil, and set aside.

Add a generous drizzle of olive oil and the butter to a large skillet and melt the butter in the oil over medium-low heat. Add the garlic and cook for about 1 minute, just until fragrant. Add the chickpeas and increase the heat to medium. Add a large pinch of salt and cook until the chickpeas are heated through and start to take on a little color, about 5 minutes. Remove from the heat and add the lemon zest, lemon juice, and a bit more olive oil if the mixture seems dry. Toss to combine and season with salt and freshly ground black pepper.

Toss the chickpea mixture with the pappardelle and finish with toasted walnuts.

SPAGHETTI WITH SARDINES, LEMON, AND ARUGULA

Sometimes we create our best meals out of necessity. I had come home, exhausted, opened up the cupboards, and found the ingredients that made up this pasta dish sitting happily in my cupboard and refrigerator. Now I shop for the ingredients with purpose because this pasta is a fresh delight that's even good cold, eaten straight out of the refrigerator.

Serves 4

1 small yellow onion, finely chopped
2 to 4 garlic cloves, finely chopped
1 (3.75-ounce / 106-g) can sardines in olive oil, bones
   and any scales removed
Zest and juice of 3 lemons
1 pound (500 g) spaghetti
Extra virgin olive oil
1 bunch flat-leaf parsley, finely chopped
Red chile flakes
Salt and freshly ground black pepper
About 3 cups (60 g) loosely packed arugula

Add a generous drizzle of olive oil to a large skillet and heat over medium heat. Add the onion and a sprinkle of salt and cook until the onion is soft and translucent, about 5 minutes. Add the garlic and stir to incorporate. Crumble the sardines and add to the onion mixture. Turn the heat up and cook until there's some golden color on the fish. Add the lemon zest and stir to combine. Turn the heat off and set aside.

Bring a large pot of salted water to a boil, add the pasta, and cook until al dente. Drain and add directly to the sardine mixture. Add the lemon juice, another generous drizzle of olive oil, and the parsley. Toss to combine, then add a sprinkle of red chile flakes and toss again. Season with salt and freshly ground black pepper. Top the pasta with the arugula, drizzle it with olive oil, and sprinkle with salt and freshly ground black pepper to serve.

VEGETABLES

I equate preparing vegetables to a bonding ritual, one that creates a sense of community through a shared task.

When I was a child spending my summers in Greece, I'd often watch the women of my family sit together with huge piles of dandelion, spinach, or amaranth greens in front of them, sorting the good leaves from the bad and clipping off the tougher stems. They did this while gossiping, occasionally/often fighting, talking in hushed tones about their children's cars or their children's wives, or both.

I would eavesdrop to see if they were talking about me—as they often were— and as I got older I would join them in their vegetable preparation, taking pleasure in their delight that someone from my generation would sit and perform what felt like a task of the past with them. With my grandmother and her sisters, I spent hours cleaning green beans and wild greens and pricking fresh olives all over with a fork so they were ready for curing.

As a teenager growing up in Boston, I remember catching my mother as she cleaned green beans by herself in our kitchen, quietly snapping off the end with the stem. I couldn't resist but sit and help her, drawn to it like it had a force field that beckoned me to the task. It didn't seem right that she would clean them by herself.

Parea, or company, is something Greek women have always called upon in order to get cooking done. Vegetables are often the main dish in Greece, and if not the main dish they are plentiful side dishes. I try to retain that attitude of company and sharing while I'm cooking them.

When my Jewish heritage from my dad's side makes its way into my cooking, the same feeling of community is infused in the cooking process. We peel the potatoes for latkes together. Even if you happen to be frying latkes alone, everyone will crowd around you to keep you company—whether you like it or not—to get one of the first piping hot latkes out of the pan.

The vegetables I cook are the star of the show—the preparation is simple, and everything else is meant to embellish their perfect outfit and shine the light a little brighter on them. Attention to detail is critical when preparing simple food. For example, boiled *horta*, or greens, are an iconic Greek vegetable eaten with most fish dishes. It's a basic dish, but the boiling water has to be heavily salted and the greens properly drained of water. Lots of olive oil and lemon juice—not to mention an additional sprinkle of salt—are key to achieving the perfect seasoning. In turn, you are rewarded with deliciousness.

I treat vegetables with the highest honor. They remind me of the generations before me gathering together to prepare food and nourish one another. They are the colorful centerpiece at the table, providing the vibrant hues I like to incorporate into every meal I cook. The correct preparation and the right amount of seasoning go a long way to creating a simple vegetable dish you want to eat again and again.

SPIGARELLO WITH OLIVE OIL AND LEMON

You can judge a well-cooked green by the lack of water on it when you eat it. Only olive oil, lemon juice, and salt should glisten on its leaves.

This simple fact makes the difference between *oohs* and *ahhs* and *how did you make this?* questions to the less appealing option of resigning oneself to eat a pile of swampy greens. My yiayia would turn up her nose at greens that were not well drained.

These greens are cooked in a pot of salted water and then placed in a colander to drain. Draining will take about 20 minutes of inactive time that is well worth the result. I love the look and texture of spigarello, which is in the broccoli family, but you can use Swiss chard, kale, spinach, beet greens, dandelion greens, amaranth greens, or any other leafy green you like.

Serves 4 to 6

2 bunches spigarello or greens of your choice
Extra virgin olive oil
Juice of 2 lemons, or to taste
Salt

In a large pot, bring 4 inches of water with a small handful of salt to a boil.

Wash and chop the greens into rough large pieces, discarding the bottom woody stems. Place in the boiling water and, using tongs, turn them over until they wilt. Cook for 4 to 5 minutes, until the greens are no longer crunchy and are easy to bite through.

Remove the greens from the water with tongs and place into a colander to drain for 20 to 30 minutes, fluffing them occasionally to let the steam escape and so they can dry out.

When you are ready to serve, place the greens on a serving plate, large enough to hold the greens in a single layer. Drizzle generously with olive oil, then the lemon juice. Sprinkle with salt and serve.

BRIAM (GREEK-STYLE ROASTED VEGETABLES WITH GRATED TOMATO AND OLIVE OIL)

Briam, fresh vegetables smothered in onions, tomatoes, and olive oil then baked until meltingly soft with crispy bits of onion and vegetables, warrants the expense of fresh, high-quality ingredients. It is that magical Greek way of cooking vegetables in lots of olive oil that makes them satisfying as the main dish.

I love making this dish in the summer; it feeds many and is perfect for a larger dinner or to have leftovers. You can eat it warm or at room temperature with some feta or Greek yogurt and fresh bread to mop up the delicious olive oil and vegetable juices.

Serves 6 to 8

1 pound (450 g) thin-skinned waxy yellow or red potatoes
1½ pounds (680 g) eggplant (any variety)
1 pound (450 g) bell peppers (any variety and size)
1 pound (450 g) zucchini
2 large yellow onions
4 garlic cloves
1 pint (300 g) cherry tomatoes (optional)
6 large tomatoes
1 cup (240 ml) extra virgin olive oil
Salt and freshly ground black pepper

Preheat the oven to 350°F (180°C). Have two 9 × 13–inch rectangular pans ready.

Cut the potatoes, eggplant, peppers, and zucchini into rustic, bite-size pieces and place in a large bowl.

Slice the onions into thin half-moons and peel and roughly chop the garlic. Toss the onions, garlic, and whole cherry tomatoes (if using) with the cut vegetables.

Over a bowl, grate the tomatoes on the large holes of a box grater. As you grate, you will be left with the peel of the tomato, which you can discard or save for another use.

Toss the vegetables with the grated tomato, the olive oil, and lots of salt and freshly ground black pepper, making sure the vegetables are well seasoned. Divide the vegetables between the two baking pans, making sure to equally divide any extra juice between both. Cover the tops with aluminum foil. Bake for 40 minutes. Increase the temperature to 400°F and remove the foil and bake for another 30 to 40 minutes, or until the vegetables are golden brown on top.

ROASTED EGGPLANT WITH TAHINI AND PINE NUTS

Eggplant, roasted with plenty of olive oil until it is golden brown and caramelized, is a dish no one should miss and everyone should know how to make. Eggplants are a bit tricky to prepare. In order for them to cook through and soften, they need generous helpings of olive oil (they are like sponges) and extra time roasting in the oven. In this dish, slices of crispy eggplant are layered over rich lemony tahini and topped with pine nuts. I like to eat this paired with roasted or grilled fish, or as a side to a platter of Oven Chickpeas (page 110).

Serves 4 to 6

For the roasted eggplant:
2 medium Italian eggplants
   (about 1½ pounds / 700 g)
About ½ cup (120 ml) extra virgin olive oil
1 garlic clove, chopped
Salt and freshly ground black pepper

For the tahini:
½ cup (120 ml) tahini
Juice of 1 lemon
¼ cup (60 ml) water
Salt

For the pine nuts:
¼ cup (45 g) raw pine nuts
Extra virgin olive oil
Salt

Chopped flat-leaf parsley or cilantro, for garnish

To make the eggplant: preheat the oven to 425°F (220°C). Line a baking sheet with parchment paper.

Cut off either end of the eggplants. Slice lengthwise down the middle and then slice into ½-inch half-moons. Place in a bowl and drizzle with enough olive oil so that every piece is saturated. This is important and will be more olive oil than you think. Toss in the garlic and add another generous drizzle of olive oil for good measure. Generously salt and pepper the eggplant slices.

Place the eggplant on the prepared baking sheet and roast until golden brown, about 30 minutes, flipping halfway through so both sides are golden. Remove from the oven.

To make the tahini: while the eggplant is in the oven, place the tahini in a bowl and whisk in the lemon juice and a generous pinch of salt. Slowly add the water, whisking the entire time, until you get the consistency of whipped cream.

To cook the pine nuts: place pine nuts in a small heavy skillet. Drizzle with enough olive oil to barely coat the nuts and sprinkle with salt. Toast over very low heat until golden brown, shaking the pan often.

To serve: spread the tahini on the bottom of a platter. Arrange the eggplant on top and sprinkle with the pine nuts and parsley or cilantro.

BATSARIA
(VINEGARED BEETS)

This simple dish is a staple on the Greek lunch table—what makes it special is that most people are surprised that you can cook the beet greens as well. The beets are boiled until soft and served with their greens for a ruby red and puckery wholesome and delicious side. Traditionally, this is served with Fried Salt Cod (page 76) and *Skordalia* (page 181), a trifecta that has stood the test of time.

Serves 4

1 bunch of red beets with their greens
1 garlic clove
Good quality red wine vinegar
Extra virgin olive oil
Salt and freshly ground black pepper

Cut the beets away from their greens and wash the beets and the greens well. Cut off the tops of beets to remove the tough gritty part that was attached to the greens.

Place the beets in a medium/large pot and fill with enough water to cover the beets completely. Add a dash of salt to the water and bring to a boil over high heat.

Reduce the heat to medium/low and simmer until the beets are very tender, about 30 to 40 minutes, depending on their size.

When you can easily pierce a beet with a knife, they are ready. Remove from heat, drain, and cover in cold water. When they have cooled, you can slide the peel off with your hands under cold water. Cut each beet into wedges and place in a bowl.

Fill the pot you boiled the beets in with an inch of water and a dash of salt. Bring to a boil and add the greens. Reduce the heat to medium/low and simmer for 3 to 5 minutes. The greens should still be green, but soft. Drain the greens, coarsely chop, and add to the beets.

To serve the beets: grate the garlic clove either on a zester or the small holes of a grater and add to the beets. Drizzle the beets generously with olive oil, red wine vinegar, and a generous sprinkle of salt and freshly ground black pepper. Toss to combine and taste for seasoning, adding more vinegar and salt to taste.

LATKES

Is there anything better than a crispy fried potato? I think not.

I have been doing the same epic Hanukkah party for ten years. I fry latkes continuously for three hours straight, feeding about a hundred hungry guests. The great result of this latke training is that I went through it so you don't have to. You can read this recipe and make latkes as they should be—perfectly crispy and salty on the outside while soft and yielding on the inside.

I like to serve latkes the traditional way —topped with sour cream and homemade applesauce—or with smoked salmon, capers, and a squeeze of lemon.

Serves 4 to 6

4 large russet potatoes (about 2 pounds / 1 kg), peeled
1 medium yellow onion, peeled and kept whole
1 egg
2 tablespoons all-purpose flour
Salt and freshly ground black pepper
Vegetable oil for frying

Grate the potatoes on the large holes of a box grater or with the grater attachment of a food processor. I find the food processor gives longer strands that are fun when frying, as they resemble shoestring fries fanning out from the latke.

Place the grated potatoes in a big bowl of cold water. Grate the onion on the large holes of the box grater and blot it on paper towels until most of the liquid is removed.

In a small bowl, whisk the egg.

When you are ready to fry the latkes, lift the potatoes out of the water and drain in a colander, pressing with a dish towel or paper towels. Get them as dry as possible. Add the grated potato to the egg, onion, and flour. Add a generous pinch of salt and lots of freshly ground black pepper.

Pour vegetable oil into a large nonstick skillet until it reaches ½ inch up the sides. When the oil is hot enough (test with a mini latke), it should happily sizzle when you put in your latkes to fry. A happy sizzle is not hot enough so that the oil splatters everywhere, but not so low that bubbles are barely forming.

Drop tablespoons of batter into the oil and wait—be patient. Don't pat the batter down too much, just a gentle press on top to even the potato is enough. Flip the latkes only when you see golden brown edges at the perimeter and try to flip only once. When golden brown on each side, remove the latkes to a plate lined with paper towels to absorb excess oil. Taste a latke and sprinkle with a little salt to finish if needed and serve hot.

GREEK FRENCH FRIES

French fries in Greece are hand-cut, fried in olive oil, and served along-side grilled and braised meats. They are also served alongside fried eggs as a lazy dinner with *maybe* the addition of a simple tomato and cucumber salad. (This meal has been my favorite since my childhood and still is to this day.) My yiayia used to fry potatoes in a rickety pot with no thermometer. She knew the oil was hot enough when she placed one French fry in the oil and it started to bubble and sizzle. Frying in olive oil can be cost-prohibitive, but it has been done for millennia and tastes absolutely divine.

I love Greek French fries, but I often avoid frying because as anyone from NYC knows, it's not easy to do here. So I've also included my oven version, which I make often and is just as light and crispy.

Serves 2 to 4

2 large russet potatoes
4 cups (960 ml) olive oil
Salt
Dried oregano (optional)

Peel the potatoes, cut into ½-inch French-fry shapes, place in a bowl filled with water, and soak for 20 to 30 minutes. Drain and pat dry.

Pour the olive oil into a medium pot and heat over medium-high heat. Test to see if the oil is ready to fry by dropping a sliced potato into the oil and seeing if it sizzles.

Fry the potatoes in batches until they are light golden brown, about 5 minutes. Using a slotted spoon, transfer the fried potatoes to a shallow bowl lined with paper towels. Generously sprinkle the fries with salt and oregano, if using, and serve.

Oven French-fry variation:
Preheat the oven to 450°F (225°C). Line a baking sheet with parchment paper. Toss the drained potatoes with ¼ cup (60 ml) olive oil. Place on the prepared baking sheet and generously sprinkle with salt and oregano, if using. Roast for 25 to 30 minutes, until golden brown. Serve hot.

KOUNOUPIDI YIAHNI (BRAISED CAULIFLOWER WITH TOMATO AND OLIVE OIL)

Yiahni roughly translates into a style and method of cooking something in a tomato, onion, and olive oil sauce. The cauliflower becomes soft and sweet while almost falling apart and the potatoes are satisfying and hearty. This dish is complete with a side of good feta and fresh bread.

Serves 4

¼ cup (60 ml) extra virgin olive oil, plus more for finishing
1 large yellow onion, sliced into thin half-moons
3 or 4 medium yukon gold potatoes, peeled and cut into quarters
1 medium head cauliflower, core and leaves removed,
   cut into large chunks
1 (28-ounce / 790-g) can whole peeled tomatoes
Salt and freshly ground black pepper

In a large pot, combine the olive oil, onion, a large pinch of salt, and lots of freshly ground black pepper and cook over medium-low heat until the onion starts to soften, about 5 minutes. Add the potatoes, cauliflower, and tomatoes. Add just enough water to loosen the mixture, about 1 cup (240 ml), and bring to a simmer. Put a lid on the pot and simmer until the cauliflower and potatoes are very soft, 45 to 60 minutes. Add another drizzle of olive oil and shake the pot to distribute. (Shaking the pot is a good trick for incorporating an ingredient into softly cooked vegetables, as mixing can make them fall apart.) Serve warm.

SPANAKORIZO (SPINACH RICE WITH DILL AND GREEN ONION)

This iconic Greek dish is the kind of comfort food that makes you live one hundred–plus years. Scallions, dill, and spinach (or any dark leafy green) are cooked with just a handful of rice that marries the ingredients together. The dish is finished with (drumroll, please) lemon juice, olive oil, and sometimes crumbled feta on top. I serve it as a main dish with a simple cucumber and tomato salad on the side.

Serves 2 to 4

2 bunches of spinach, about 5 cups (150 g) chopped, or 2 bunches
  of Swiss chard (trimmed of tough stems and chopped)
1 bunch scallions, white and light green parts only, chopped
1 bunch fresh dill, finely chopped, divided
½ cup (100 g) jasmine rice, rinsed
1 cup (240 ml) water
Juice of 1 lemon
Extra virgin olive oil
Salt and freshly ground black pepper

Bring a pot of salted water to a boil, add the spinach, and cook until just wilted, about 2 minutes (4 to 5 minutes for chard). Drain in a colander and set aside.

In a large pot, cook the scallions over medium-low heat with enough olive oil to generously coat them and a generous pinch of salt. Add half of the chopped dill. When the scallions and dill are soft, add the rice and cook, stirring, for 1 minute to coat in oil. Add the cooked greens, water, and another drizzle of olive oil and stir well. Cover the pot and cook until the rice is tender and the liquid is mostly absorbed, about 12 to 15 minutes. Add the lemon juice, stir, and season with salt and freshly ground black pepper.

Add a generous pour of olive oil to the dish, garnish with the rest of the dill, and serve.

BRAISED RED CABBAGE WITH APPLES

My friend Peter Regli showed me how to make this Swiss cabbage dish.
I love it as an alternative to the crispy raw cabbage I usually lean in to.
This is a sweet and sour vegetable dish, very tender and delicious with a
splash of balsamic vinegar that's reduced to a thick syrup. It's a perfect
side to a fall or winter meal of roasted sausage and a green salad.

Serves 4 to 6

2 tablespoons (30 g) butter
1 medium red onion, sliced into thin half-moons
1 medium head red cabbage quartered, cored, and thinly sliced
1 apple (any kind) skin on, cored and grated
¼ cup (60 ml) good-quality balsamic vinegar
Extra virgin olive oil
Salt and freshly ground black pepper

In a large skillet, melt the butter over medium heat and add a drizzle of
olive oil. Add the onion and cook until it wilts. Add the cabbage and toss
to combine. Add the apple and a generous pinch of salt. Cook the cabbage
and as it starts to wilt, add a splash of water if necessary to keep it wilting
and cooking without browning. Cover and cook for 15 more minutes. Add
the vinegar and toss with the cabbage. Cover again and cook, tossing
occasionally, until the cabbage is very soft, another 10 to 15 minutes. Taste
for seasoning and add salt and freshly ground black pepper as needed.

SKORDALIA
(GREEK POTATO AND GARLIC SAUCE)

Skordalia rides the line between a dip, a sauce, and a side dish. Potatoes emulsified with lots of garlic and olive oil and a splash of lemon really pack a punch of flavor. This garlicky mess of fun is a traditional Greek accompaniment to battered and fried salt cod. My yiayia would make a batch and keep it in the refrigerator all week, scooping it out as a side to anything she saw fit, from meats to fish, or serving it as a dip with fresh bread. Fried Salt Cod (page 76) and vinegary beets are favorite accompaniments of mine. I make *skordalia* the way it should be—almost spicy with garlic. It is the spirit of this dish to burn just a little—though I know that some Greeks use much more garlic than I do!

Serves 6

4 large russet potatoes (about 2 pounds / 1 kg)
1 cup (240 ml) extra virgin olive oil
3 or more garlic cloves, grated on a Microplane
Juice of 1 lemon, or more to taste
Salt

Peel the potatoes and cut into bite-size pieces. Add to a large pot of salted water and bring to a boil. Reduce the heat and cook the potatoes until very tender, 15 to 20 minutes.

Reserve ½ cup (120 ml) of the cooking water and drain the rest from the potatoes.

Place the potatoes in a large bowl and mash with the olive oil, cooking water, garlic, lemon juice, and salt. The potatoes should be very soft and easy to mash with the back of a spoon or the bottom of a glass. Add some of the reserved water to loosen the mixture if necessary. The texture should be looser than mashed potatoes and nice and green from all the olive oil.

BEETS AND CARROTS OVER YOGURT WITH MINT

One early spring I found myself in Glasgow, Scotland. My colleague Natasha and I were there to cook dinner for sixty people at the Modern Institute. We had a crash course in Scottish fare, hitting shops and farmers' markets the second we got off the plane. The cloudy beauty of the city, studded with markets, touted some of the most amazing cheese, vegetables, meat, and dairy I've ever had. The Mediterranean is deep in my blood, but now Scotland has a special place in my heart. This recipe showcases the fresh and seasonal vegetables we encountered on our trip. The rich, thick yogurt is the perfect balance to the sweetness of the carrots and beets and it is also a great dish for a crowd, as you can prep the vegetables in advance.

Serves 6 to 8

1½ pounds (680 g) red or golden beets, or a mix (about 4 medium)
1½ pounds (680 g) carrots (6 to 8 medium/large)
2 cups (560 g) plain whole milk Greek yogurt
Extra virgin olive oil
Juice of 1 lemon, or more to taste
Salt and freshly ground black pepper
1 handful mint leaves, for garnish

Scrub the beets, place them in a large pot of salted water, and bring to a boil. Lower the heat and simmer until very soft, about 45 minutes. Remove from the water, cool, then peel and slice into bite-size wedges.

Meanwhile, place the carrots in another large pot of salted water and bring to a boil. Lower the heat and simmer until soft, about 10 minutes. Remove from the water, cool, then slice into ¼-inch rounds.

Spread the yogurt over a large platter in a thick layer. Place the beets and carrots on top of the yogurt, alternating between the two. Drizzle with lots of olive oil and the lemon juice. Sprinkle generously with salt and freshly ground black pepper and finish with the mint leaves.

SIMPLE ROASTED PEPPERS WITH OLIVE OIL AND SALT

Sometimes I forget how delicious a roasted pepper can be. As an appetizer, as a side, cold from the fridge, or in a sandwich. I forget and then I remember and make a batch of peppers to have on hand. These are great just with olive oil and salt but also lovely with a sprinkling of red wine vinegar or fresh lemon juice. Feel free to use any peppers you find that look delicious.

Serves 4 to 6

15 small bell peppers or peppers of your choice
Extra virgin olive oil
Salt and freshly ground black pepper

Preheat the oven to 425°F (220°C).

Place the peppers on a baking sheet, drizzle generously with olive oil, and sprinkle generously with salt and freshly ground black pepper. Roast for 30 to 40 minutes, until the peppers start to color to a deep golden brown and are charred in spots.

Remove from the oven and allow to cool. Serve as is and let your guests sort them out, or you can open them up and clean out the seeds and stems. You can keep the peppers in the refrigerator for up to 1 week and use them as a part of meze spread or sandwich addition.

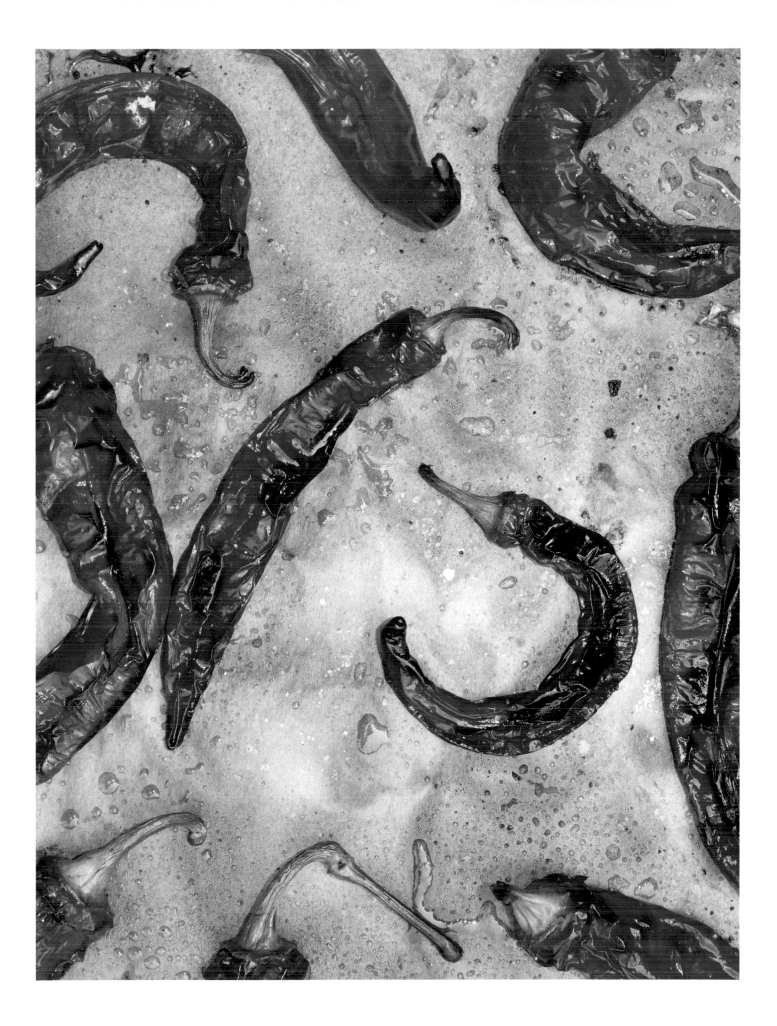

ROASTED SWEET POTATOES WITH GREEK YOGURT, PISTACHIOS, AND CILANTRO

My instinct is to always prepare vegetables simply, but these sweet potatoes are my dressed-up version when I want something a little more complex that also looks beautiful on the plate. This fall dish offers layers of flavor and texture—tangy, sweet, crunchy, and herbaceous—all my favorite things on one plate and in one mouthful. These sweet potatoes are nice served with Braised Chickpeas with Orange Zest and Garlic Breadcrumbs (page 114) and a green salad.

Serves 4 to 6

4 small to medium sweet potatoes, cut in half lengthwise
2 tablespoons extra virgin olive oil, plus more for drizzling
1½ cups (330 g) plain whole or 2% Greek yogurt
Juice of 1 lemon or lime
½ cup (60 g) raw pistachios, chopped, for garnish
1 handful cilantro, chopped, for garnish
Salt and freshly ground black pepper

Preheat the oven to 400°F (200°C). Line a baking sheet with parchment paper.

Drizzle the sweet potatoes with olive oil so the entire half has a nice sheen on it. Sprinkle the sweet potatoes with salt and place them cut-side down on the sheet.

Roast for 30 to 40 minutes, until the sweet potatoes are cooked through and have puffy brown spots on them. Place faceup on a serving platter and allow to cool until they are just warm.

In a medium bowl, whisk the yogurt with the lemon juice and 2 tablespoons olive oil and season with salt. Dollop a spoonful on each sweet potato and garnish with the pistachios and cilantro. Drizzle with olive oil and freshly ground black pepper.

DESSERT

I used to work in ice cream. It was my first "real" job after my formative middle school years of dog walking and babysitting. I was fourteen years old and ready for independence.

I walked into my favorite ice cream shop, Rancatore's, in Belmont, Massachusetts, and applied for a job. I went to Rancatore's at least a few times a week with my father, who exhibited vast amounts of patience when confronted with his daughter's ice cream addiction.

I loved this job *so much*. I haven't liked a job as much since then. I would sign up for double shifts whenever I could and relished in the long lines of customers in the summer. I watched when Joe, the owner, would make the ice cream every day, the ice cream machine churning out all different kinds of flavors—bittersweet chocolate, French vanilla, Hydrox Cookie, and ginger, to name a few.

I never got sick of it. The job and the ice cream both. I looked forward to my shifts as if I was going to the world's most fun and exclusive party, and I would plan which two flavors would be my daily dose, like pairing a designer outfit with the right shoes.

I learned how to use a cash register, make coffee, scoop ice cream like a pro, and, most important, Joe taught me how to mop. On my first day of training, as we were closing down the shop, Joe took one look at me trying to wield the industrial mop across the sticky, ice cream–covered floor and gave me one of life's most important lessons: mopping should be effortless.

You start at one end of the floor and waltz to the next, your hands doing a slight twisty motion as you slowly walk backward. Don't push too hard, just follow the lead of those heavy, soapy cotton strands and let them do the work for you. I've never mopped the same way since.

I have applied this analogy of effortlessness to so many things in life that my friends often roll their eyes and groan when I bring up my beloved high school job. But it is true, right? Effortlessness is a job well done, an outcome of its fullest expression.

This memory came to mind as I was thinking about dessert . . . mostly because I often think about how much I love ice cream. And then I think about how the best things come from understanding what you are working with and allowing it to do the work for you.

I don't like fussy cooking and I'm not a patient and precise baker. I like easy, flavorful desserts that are not too sweet. I like ice cream in any form—soft serve with sprinkles, scoops of ice cream, ice cream cakes. Moist syrupy Greek phyllo cakes, cookies, doughnuts, and puddings. I also occasionally like simple, cut-up seasonal fruits with chunks of good chocolate or an easy cream. Dessert should taste effortless, a peaceful and satisfying end to the meal.

PERSIAN FIGS WITH CARDAMOM AND ROSEWATER

My obsession with preserving Persian-style figs started with my friend Atossa and her mother, Shahla. Atossa came over for dinner one night and brought a magical gift her mother had made—a jar of preserved purple figs that were served with spoonfuls of thick Greek yogurt for dessert. I had never had anything like it before and immediately started asking her many questions about how to re-create the Persian fig magic.

I learned that the magic happens as figs are simmered in sugar, water, cardamom, and rosewater. Caramel notes and the fragrance of cardamom and rose add a welcome assault on the senses. These delights can also be served on their own or with a fresh cheese.

Makes 2 quarts

2 pints fresh figs (about 1 pound / 480 g)
2½ cups (600 ml) water
1½ cups (300 g) granulated sugar
¼ teaspoon salt
8 whole cardamom pods
2 tablespoons rosewater

Prick the figs halfway through with a fork 3 or 4 times. Place in a medium pot with the water, sugar, salt, cardamom pods, and rosewater. Bring to a boil over high heat, then reduce the heat to low and simmer until the figs are soft and the liquid is syrupy, about 45 minutes. As the figs cook, gently shake the pot to redistribute the figs and syrup. When the figs are done, remove from the heat and place into clean glass jars submerged in the syrup. They will keep, refrigerated, for up to 1 month.

BUTTERSCOTCH PUDDING WITH WHIPPED CREAM AND TOASTED PECANS

Brown sugar and butter are the primary ingredients of butterscotch. The term *scotch* in butterscotch is a disputed terminology—it either refers to its country of origin (Scotland) or the fact that oftentimes the butter is "scotched," or scorched, to make the confection. Regardless of its origins, it is one of my favorite flavors (because it reminds me of salted caramel ice cream).

This is the perfect dessert for large groups, because it is consistently delicious and easily made in large batches (just double or triple the recipe).

Serves 6 to 8

For the pudding:
¼ cup (60 g) butter
3 cups (700 ml) whole milk
2 egg yolks, beaten
1 teaspoon vanilla extract
1 teaspoon kosher salt
1 cup (200 g) dark brown sugar
¼ cup (30 g) cornstarch

For the whipped cream:
2 cups (480 ml) heavy cream
1 tablespoon maple syrup

To garnish:
1 cup (140 g) pecans, toasted (see page 9)
  and chopped

In a small saucepan, heat the butter over medium-low heat until it melts and turns light brown. It will get frothy, and once the froth subsides, it will start browning. Watch it closely and remove it from the heat once you see brown bits forming on the bottom. Set aside.

In a large bowl, whisk together the milk, egg yolks, vanilla, and salt and set aside. In a medium nonstick pot, combine the brown sugar and cornstarch. Place over medium heat, whisk, then whisk in the egg and milk mixture. Cook, whisking constantly, for 8 to 10 minutes, until the mixture thickens and coats the back of a spoon. Remove from the heat and whisk in the brown butter.

Ladle the pudding into little glasses or ramekins. Cover with plastic wrap directly touching the pudding so it does not form a skin, transfer to the refrigerator, and chill for at least 1 hour. (Alternatively, chill in a large bowl.) This can be made up to two days in advance. When you are ready to serve, beat the cream with the maple syrup using an electric mixer until soft peaks form (if making in advance, chill until ready to serve). Top the pudding with the barely sweetened whipped cream and toasted pecans.

ICE CREAM CAKE

Ice cream cake is the eighth wonder of the world. It is a very simple process that involves no actual skill, yet it seems to impress people and it is probably the most exciting dessert imaginable. There is no birthday cake that can top *the* ice cream cake. I am a traditionalist: the cake should be layers of ice cream with an Oreo cookie crust and slathered in homemade whipped cream. Leave it plain or top it with flowers, sprinkles, or decorations of your choice. I think homemade ice cream cake should look a little messy, not perfect, and a little lopsided. The only special equipment you need is a springform pan so you can get the cake out of the pan.

Serves 10 to 12

For the crust:
2 tablespoons (30 g) melted butter, plus
    softened butter for the pan
15 Oreo cookies (180 g)

For the cake:
4 pints ice cream, slightly softened
    (2 vanilla and 2 chocolate or any
    combination you like)

For the fillings and toppings:
Anything your heart desires: crushed Oreos, toasted
    almonds, sprinkles, chocolate chips, M&M's
    (my favorite is crushed Oreos and toasted almonds)

For the whipped cream:
2 cups (480 ml) heavy cream
1 tablespoon maple syrup

Butter the bottom of a 9-inch springform pan and line it with a round of parchment paper.

Pulse the Oreo cookies in a food processor with the melted butter until the crumbs come together. Press the crumbs into the bottom of the springform pan and up the sides just a bit. Gently press one flavor of ice cream on top of the cookie crust and smooth with the back of a spoon. I try to evenly drop "blobs" of ice cream before smoothing it out. Sprinkle the filling of your choice over the ice cream and place the cake in the freezer for 15 minutes to chill before you continue with the second layer of ice cream.

Remove the cake from the freezer and add the second layer of ice cream, smoothing it with the back of the spoon so the top is flat.

Place the cake back in the freezer and chill for at least 2 hours, until the cake is totally frozen, so you are able to frost it with the whipped cream. Using an electric mixer, whip the heavy cream and maple syrup until stiff peaks form.

Remove the cake from the freezer and remove it from the springform pan. I like to do this by holding a knife under hot water and running it as best as possible around the sides.

Place the cake on a plate or a platter (that fits in your freezer) and cover the sides and top with the whipped cream. Sprinkle with topping of your choice and put the cake back in the freezer for at least 2 hours, or until you are ready to serve. The ice cream cake is best when it sits in the refrigerator for 30 minutes before serving.

PORTOKALOPITA (SYRUP-SOAKED ORANGE PHYLLO CAKE)

The word *portokalopita*, a Greek dessert literally meaning "orange pie," made its debut appearance in the *New York Times* Sunday Styles section on September 19, 2011. It was a story before the opening of the restaurant at PS1 called "How to Throw a Romantic Greek Dinner Party." I learned how to make this fruity, syrupy sweet in the mountainous village of Karpenisi in central Greece. The woman who shared the recipe with me, an unassuming and humble cook with a small taverna in the village, should be applauded for this simple and delightful dessert. Phyllo is shredded and mixed into a yogurt batter that is then baked. When it comes out of the oven it is soaked in an orangey syrup that makes for pure joy in every juicy, spongy bite.

Serves 10 to 12

For the syrup:
2 cups (480 ml) water
2 cups (400 g) granulated sugar
6 strips orange peel
2 cinnamon sticks
1 teaspoon kosher salt

For the cake pudding:
½ cup (120 ml) canola or safflower oil,
   plus more for the pan
3 eggs
1 (7-ounce / 200-g) container plain Greek yogurt
½ cup (100 g) granulated sugar
1 teaspoon vanilla extract
2½ teaspoons baking powder
1 (1-pound / 454-g) package phyllo dough

To make the syrup: combine all the syrup ingredients in a pot and bring to a simmer over medium/low heat. Simmer for 5 minutes for the ingredients to meld. Remove from the heat and set aside to cool.

To make the cake: preheat the oven to 350°F (180°C) and oil a 9-inch cake pan.

In a large bowl, whisk the eggs, yogurt, canola oil, sugar, vanilla, and baking powder.

Shred the phyllo into pieces and fluff with your fingers to separate the pieces. Fold the phyllo pieces into the yogurt mixture and use your fingers to make sure every piece of phyllo is covered in the batter.

Pour the batter into the prepared pan and bake for 45 minutes, or until golden brown on top. Remove the cake from the oven and poke it with a fork or chopstick all over the place so you have lots of holes for the syrup to soak in. Slowly pour the syrup over the hot cake. You might have to pause midway through and wait for the cake to absorb the syrup before adding more. It will seem like a lot of syrup, but trust me, use all of it or the cake will be dry. Let the cake sit for at least 1 hour before serving.

The cake is best served warm or at room temperature the day you make it. Store leftovers in an airtight container for up to 3 days.

SUPER LEMONY OLIVE OIL CAKE
A SPIN ON THE CLASSIC

At the café we hover between a surplus of oranges and a surplus of lemons, depending on which day of the week it is.

My original recipe for olive oil cake uses orange juice and orange zest, which is very traditionally Greek and exceptionally fragrant. One day, when we ran out of oranges at the café—and making the original recipe meant wasting precious time going to the grocery store—we made it with lemons.

It was anything but disappointing. In fact, now I don't know which version I like better. This olive oil cake is lemony and creamy, and one of my favorite things about the cake is its color. When you dive past the crunchy, golden brown exterior, you are met with a soft, light yellow interior that tastes divine. Olive oil and lemon—always a heavenly match!

Serves 10 to 12

1½ cups (350 ml) extra virgin olive oil,
   plus more for the pan
3 eggs
1¼ cups (250 g) plus 1 tablespoon granulated sugar
1¼ cups (295 ml) whole milk
Juice and zest of 2 lemons
2 teaspoons vanilla extract

2 cups (240 g) all-purpose flour
½ teaspoon baking soda
½ teaspoon baking powder
1 teaspoon salt
Powdered sugar for serving

Preheat the oven to 350°F (180°C). Lightly oil a 9-inch springform cake pan, line the bottom with a round of parchment paper, and oil again.

In a large bowl, whisk together the eggs, olive oil, and sugar until smooth. Whisk in the milk, lemon zest, lemon juice, and vanilla.

In a separate bowl, whisk the flour, baking soda, baking powder, and salt. Make a well in the middle of the flour mixture and slowly pour in the olive oil mixture, whisking to combine. Start with small circles that get larger as you incorporate more dry and wet batter.

Whisk until mostly smooth—some lumps are OK. Pour the batter into the prepared pan and sprinkle with the remaining 1 tablespoon sugar.

Bake for 50 minutes, or until the top is golden brown and a toothpick inserted in the middle of the cake comes out clean. Allow the cake to cool and serve at room temperature garnished with powdered sugar and extra lemon zest if you have it.

SEMOLINA HALVAH WITH TOASTED ALMONDS AND CINNAMON

This dessert is proudly passed down from generation to generation—it's very easy to make, and so incredibly delicious. My yiayia's neighbor Kiria Dimitra taught me her variation, and it is the one most familiar and nostalgic to me. She would slice it thick and top it with a dusting of cinnamon every time we would come visit.

Halvah—a pudding of toasted semolina mixed with olive oil and syrup and then cooled and served sliced—is steeped in historical significance. This traditional treat of the Middle East and Greece has many variations from region to region and country to country.

This dessert is a great example of simplicity being culinary perfection. The only hitch is you *must* use a high-quality extra virgin olive oil because it will make all the difference in flavor. The traditional sugar measurement is a bit too sweet for me, so I reduced it, but feel free to adjust it to your taste. Desserts in Greece and the Middle East are often incredibly sweet and meant to be served with strong coffee or tea.

Serves 10 to 12

2½ cups (600 ml) granulated sugar
4 cups (960 ml) water
2 cinnamon sticks
1 teaspoon salt
1 cup (240 ml) extra virgin olive oil,
   plus more for the pan

2 cups (340 g) coarse semolina
1 cup (145 g) whole blanched almonds, toasted
   (see page 9) and chopped
Ground cinnamon for dusting

Lightly oil a 10-cup Bundt pan or 9 × 11–inch rectangular pan.

In a medium saucepan, combine the sugar, water, cinnamon sticks, and salt. Bring to a simmer over medium heat, then reduce the heat to medium-low and heat for 7 minutes. Discard the cinnamon sticks and set aside the syrup while you prepare the semolina.

Pour the olive oil into a large pot and heat over medium-low heat for 30 seconds. Add the semolina and mix well. Cook, mixing all the while, for 6 to 7 minutes, until it's nicely toasted and golden brown. At first it will have the consistency of wet sand and then it will get softer. Ladle in the syrup a few at a time, mixing constantly. Cook for about 5 minutes, or until it gets thick and forms big bubbles. (Be careful, it tends to splatter!) Remove from heat and mix in ¾ cup (72 g) of the toasted almonds.

Spoon the hot halvah into the prepared pan and smooth the top. Cool completely, at least 1 hour. If using a Bundt pan, invert onto a platter and cover with the chopped almonds and a heavy dusting of cinnamon. If using a rectangular pan, cut into diamonds and sprinkle each piece with a few of the remaining almonds and dust with cinnamon. This keeps for three days in an airtight container.

STICKY CINNAMON DATE CAKE

This cake is based on the traditional British dessert sticky toffee pudding. My version incorporates more of a Middle Eastern flair—I use extra dates and add a good dose of cinnamon to amplify the flavors I love. A bite of this moist cinnamon date cake soaked in toffee sauce is everything dessert should be. And with a scoop of vanilla ice cream it's simply perfection.

For the toffee sauce:
2 cups (480 ml) heavy cream
½ cup (100 g) light brown sugar
½ teaspoon salt
1 teaspoon vanilla extract

For the cake:
1¼ cups (150 g) all-purpose flour
1 teaspoon baking powder
2 teaspoons ground cinnamon

½ teaspoon salt
8 ounces (225 g) dried Medjool dates, pitted
1 cup (240 ml) water
1 teaspoon baking soda
½ cup (100 g) granulated sugar
4 tablespoons (60 g) butter, at room temperature, plus more for the pan
2 eggs at room temperature
1 teaspoon vanilla extract

Preheat the oven to 350°F (180°C) and butter a 9-inch round cake pan.

To make the toffee sauce: in a medium saucepan set over medium heat, whisk together the cream, brown sugar, salt, and vanilla until the mixture comes to a simmer. Turn the heat down to low and cook, continuing to whisk, for 5 minutes or so, until it thickens up a little. Keep in mind the sauce will still remain loose. Pour half of the sauce into the cake pan and place in the freezer for 5 minutes.

Cover the rest of the sauce with plastic wrap directly on the surface so it doesn't form a skin and set aside.

To make the cake: in a small bowl, mix together the flour, baking powder, cinnamon, and salt.

In a medium saucepan, heat the dates and water over medium/high heat. Once the mixture comes to a boil, remove from the heat and mix in the baking soda. Place the date mixture in a blender and blend until almost smooth—leaving it a little chunky adds nice texture. Set aside.

In a large bowl, whisk together the sugar and butter until combined. Add the eggs one at a time, the vanilla extract, and whisk to combine. Add the date mixture and whisk until incorporated. Add the flour mixture and whisk until the batter is nice and smooth.

Pour the batter into the prepared cake pan (the sauce might rise up the sides, which is OK) and bake for 35 to 40 minutes, until a toothpick comes out clean.

Serve the cake warm with extra toffee sauce spooned over the top and a dusting of cinnamon.

LOUKOUMADES (GREEK DOUGHNUTS WITH WALNUTS AND MAPLE SYRUP)

Alex and I made a ritual of frying these traditional Greek doughnuts, or *loukoumades*, at the Gavin Brown Christmas party every year back when the gallery was in the West Village and the parties were fun, loud, and the sea of people hard to walk through. It gave us something to do at the party right around the time we started to feel restless, around 12 a.m. We would heat a vat of vegetable oil, fry these delightful puffs, and pass them out hot, covered in maple syrup and salty toasted walnuts. Traditionally they are drizzled with honey, but I prefer the natural caramel quality of maple syrup for these treats.

1 (¼-ounce / 7-g) packet active dry yeast or
  2¼ teaspoons (7 g) instant dried yeast
½ cup (120 ml) lukewarm water
2 teaspoons granulated sugar
½ cup (120 ml) whole milk, at room temperature
1½ cups (180 g) all-purpose flour
½ teaspoon salt
2 tablespoons extra olive oil
Vegetable or canola oil for frying

Garnishes:
Maple syrup
Walnuts, toasted (see page 9) and finely chopped
Ground cinnamon
Flaky salt such as Maldon (optional)

In a large bowl, combine the yeast, lukewarm water, and sugar and let stand for 5 minutes, or until frothy. Add the milk, flour, salt, and olive oil and whisk well to combine. Cover with plastic wrap and set aside for 1½ hours, or until the mixture doubles in size.

Pour vegetable oil into a medium pot to come 4 inches up the sides. Heat over medium-high heat. Line a plate with paper towels. To see if the oil is hot and ready to fry, drop in a small spoonful of batter. If it is ready, it will sizzle immediately and bubbles will form.

Drop generous tablespoons of the batter in the hot oil 4 or 5 at a time. Gently turn them with a spoon and fry until they are golden brown and puffy. (Careful of the hot oil! Turn the heat down if it's bubbling and splattering too much.) With a slotted spoon, remove the doughnuts to the paper towel–lined plate. When you are finished frying the doughnuts, place them in a bowl and drizzle with maple syrup until they have a nice coat. Shake the bowl forward and backward—try to flip the doughnuts so they are all evenly coated. Cover with the walnuts and dust the top with cinnamon and just a little pinch of salt, if using, and serve warm.

CAJETA DE COCO
(COSTA RICAN COCONUT FUDGE)

Around holidays I make big snowy piles of this sweet Central American coconut treat. They are devoured with joy at every party because they taste like a delightful ball of dulce de leche with a coconut twist. You can never have too many on hand, because they make people so happy. I like to use salted butter in this recipe to balance out the sweetness. If you have unsalted butter you can use that instead, adding ½ teaspoon of kosher salt. They are best slightly chilled but delicious at room temperature as well.

Makes 25 to 30 balls

2 cups (480 ml) sweetened condensed milk
2 cups (200 g) unsweetened shredded coconut, divided
1 cup (225 g) salted butter
1 cup (100 g) graham cracker crumbs
½ teaspoon vanilla extract

Combine the sweetened condensed milk, 1 cup (100 g) of the coconut, the butter, graham cracker crumbs, and vanilla in a medium saucepan. Bring to a boil over medium heat, stirring constantly. Lower the heat a little and simmer for an additional 5 minutes, or until it comes together and you can see the bottom of the pan when you stir. Remove from the heat, transfer to a bowl, and let the mixture cool down completely. Form the mixture into balls a teaspoonful at a time. Place the remaining 1 cup (100 g) coconut into a small skillet. Toast over medium heat, stirring, until it just starts to brown. Transfer to a plate to cool, then roll the balls in the toasted coconut and they are ready to eat.

These will keep in the refrigerator in an airtight container for up to 2 weeks.

CHOCOLATE OLIVE OIL COOKIES WITH SEA SALT

I love the combination of olive oil and chocolate. In this recipe, the olive oil creates a silky, rich texture and enhances the flavor of the dark chocolate. Topping the cookies with a touch of sea salt perfectly offsets their sweetness and makes them sparkle.

Makes about 3 dozen cookies

¾ cup (240 ml) extra virgin olive oil
1 cup (200 g) granulated sugar
2 eggs
2 teaspoons vanilla extract
2 cups (240 g) all-purpose flour
⅔ cup (65 g) cocoa powder
¾ teaspoon baking soda
½ teaspoon kosher salt
2 (3-ounce / 170-g) dark chocolate bars, chopped into fine irregular bite-size shards and the other chopped in medium shards for garnishing the cookies
Flaky salt, such as Maldon, for garnish

Preheat the oven to 350°F (180°C). Line two baking sheets with parchment paper.

In a large bowl, whisk together the olive oil and sugar. Add the eggs and vanilla extract and whisk again until everything is incorporated.

In a medium bowl, whisk together the flour, cocoa powder, baking soda, and kosher salt.

Add the flour mixture to the olive oil mixture and mix until combined. Add the finely chopped chocolate bar and fold in to combine. Cover and chill the cookie dough for 1 hour.

Scoop the dough with a tablespoon and drop onto the prepared cookie sheets. Gently indent the middle of each cookie and place a medium chopped chocolate shard in the middle. Sprinkle a little flaky salt on each cookie.

Bake the cookies for 7 to 8 minutes. I prefer them slightly undercooked so they are nice and soft. Allow the cookies to cool on the baking sheet and then remove to a serving plate. The cookies keep in an airtight container for 1 week.

SIMPLE DESSERT PLATES

These are three desserts I make often. They're platters I put together when I'm cooking for a crowd and want to avoid baking in large quantities. They work well when a simple, unfussy dessert is called for.

These dessert plates are also a nod to the seasons, celebrating produce at its best and making the most of the varieties and beautiful colors of fruit.

CITRUS AND CHOCOLATE

In winter, when citrus of all different kinds is available, I cut different colored oranges such as navel, blood, and Cara Cara into wedges and put them on a plate. In between the orange slices I nestle chunks of chocolate. Weaving mint sprigs and kumquats or passion fruit into the plate is a beautiful addition.

Serves 6 to 8

3 or 4 mixed oranges, such as Cara Cara, navel, and blood oranges
1 dark and 1 milk chocolate bar
Fresh mint sprigs (optional)
Kumquats or passion fruit (optional)

Slice the oranges into 4 wedges and place peel-side down (with the "smile" facing up) on a large platter. Break pieces of chocolate into shards and place in between the oranges. If using kumquats, you can leave them whole or slice in half. If using passion fruit, slice into wedges or half-moons. Weave sprigs of fresh mint throughout the fruit and serve.

APPLES, HONEY, AND CINNAMON

This is a favorite treat from Rosh Hashanah, the Jewish holiday celebrating the New Year. I like any recipe that easily combines my two heritages. Seasonal apples, drizzled with thick spoonfuls of Greek honey, finished with a dusting of spicy, aromatic cinnamon, and that little sprinkle of salt makes it nature's salted caramel to happily usher in a sweet New Year.

Serves 6 to 8

3 or 4 apples, cored and sliced
Honey, preferably Greek
Ground cinnamon
Flaky salt, such as Maldon

Arrange the apple slices on a platter. Drizzle generously with honey, dust with cinnamon, and sprinkle on a little flaky salt.

MACERATED STRAWBERRIES AND CINNAMON MASCARPONE

This dish is an ode to my mom, who always macerates strawberries in Mavrodaphne (a sweet, fortified Greek wine) and sugar. I would be assaulted with the candylike smell of summertime strawberries she kept in a bowl. Because Mavrodaphne isn't easy to find, I macerate the strawberries in lemon juice and sugar instead. On the side I serve a simple cinnamon mascarpone to dip them in—my Greek version of strawberries and cream.

Serves 4 to 6

For the macerated strawberries:
1 (16-ounce/400-g) container strawberries, hulled and sliced in half
Juice of ½ lemon (about 1 tablespoon)
1 tablespoon granulated sugar, or more to taste

For the cinnamon mascarpone:
1 teaspoon ground cinnamon
1 tablespoon maple syrup
1 (16 ounce/453-g) container mascarpone

In a large bowl, gently mix the strawberries with the lemon juice and sugar. Cover and set aside to macerate for at least 30 minutes or up to 6 hours. In a medium bowl, mix the cinnamon and maple syrup into the mascarpone. Serve the strawberries in a bowl or on a platter with the mascarpone on the side.

BREAKFAST

Breakfast means three things to me: my home on the weekend, some favorite menu items at the café, and days when two breakfasts feels like the only way to go.

At home, breakfast takes place on the weekends, when there is more time to luxuriate. I'm guilty of partaking in the Greek habit of coffee only as my breakfast on most days.

If I do eat something in the morning, it has to be a natural pairing to my coffee and is usually of the health food nature—salty and sweet olive oil maple granola, hearty oatmeal banana pancakes with maple syrup and a generous dusting of cinnamon, or a couple of aromatic tahini biscuits—the kind my yiayia used to make.

The café, on the other hand, makes me think about all the people—like me—who usually skip breakfast and might prefer lunch foods as a late breakfast. I think this is called brunch. I imagine this to be savory, in the form of a *muhammara*-slathered toast with a soft egg and arugula. Or, my favorite, a spinach pie inspired by the irresistible coiled version that I buy every time I visit my go-to Greek grocery store in Astoria, Queens.

And then there are the meals for the days when you want to have it all. One of my best friends, Daphne, was a champion of the "two breakfasts kind of day" (which for her was a concept she applied to every day). This entails having something sweet upon waking up and something savory a few hours later—while still leaving plenty of time to also have a regular lunch.

On days when eating is a full-time job, I like to start with a bowl of granola, move to a twisty spinach pie, and then a *muhammara* toast for lunch, all the while thinking "Daphne would approve."

Even though breakfast is practically a special occasion for me, I love it. It means the weekend has arrived and it's time to relax and make sure that my cup of coffee has a companion. This section contains all the dishes I enjoy eating for breakfast. A few are items we serve at the café for brunch, and a few are dishes I grew up with that are very Greek and that I cherish as a morning treat or an afternoon snack.

GREEK FRAPPE

The Greeks have made iced instant coffee into a fine art, and I am proud to see the frappe on our menu at PS1. Everyone who tries the frappe loves the frappe, and it is a part of daily coffee culture in Greece. It is served three ways: not sweet, medium sweet, and very sweet. Medium sweet is my favorite, and that's what this recipe makes. You can adjust the sugar to where you like it.

Serves 1

1 heaping teaspoon Nescafé instant coffee
2 teaspoons granulated sugar
¾ cup (240 ml) plus a splash of water
Ice
Whole or evaporated milk

In a blender or a jar with a lid, combine the instant coffee and sugar. Add a splash of water and stir it to dissolve the sugar and coffee. Add the ¾ cup (240 ml) water and place the lid on the jar. Shake vigorously and a nice caramel-colored foam will form on top. Pour over ice and add milk to taste.

SALTY AND SWEET OLIVE OIL MAPLE GRANOLA WITH VANILLA COCONUT MILK AND BLUEBERRIES

This granola is full of flavor: not too sweet, savory from the toasted nuts, and rich from the olive oil and aromatic spices of cinnamon and cloves. My idea was to put all of the flavors of baklava into the granola. I make this at home often, and eat it with fresh blueberries. When we make it at the café, we jazz it up with creamy vanilla coconut milk and barely sweet blueberry compote. I included those recipes here, in case you feel like bringing the café to your house.

For the granola: (makes about 5 cups)
4 cups (360 g) rolled oats
1 cup (250 ml) extra virgin olive oil
¾ cup (250 ml) maple syrup
1 teaspoon vanilla extract
4 teaspoons ground cinnamon
½ teaspoon ground cloves
2 teaspoons kosher salt
1 cup (145 g) raw almonds, coarsely chopped

To make the granola: preheat the oven to 325°F (170°C). Line a baking sheet with parchment paper. In a large bowl, mix the rolled oats with the olive oil, maple syrup, vanilla extract, cinnamon, cloves, salt, and almonds. Toss until everything is incorporated and the oats are evenly coated in the olive oil and syrup. Spread evenly on the prepared baking sheet. Bake for 35 to 45 minutes, occasionally stirring the granola, until everything is golden brown. The granola will be bubbling while cooking, which is what you want. Allow to fully cool before storing. The granola keeps for 2 weeks in an airtight container.

For the vanilla coconut milk:
(makes about 5½ cups)
1 (13.5-ounce / 398-ml) can full-fat coconut milk
1 quart (946 ml) coconut milk beverage (next to the nut milks in the grocery store)
1 teaspoon vanilla extract

To make the vanilla coconut milk: in a large container, whisk the coconut milk, coconut beverage, and vanilla. The coconut milk will keep in the refrigerator for up to 10 days. Shake before serving.

For the blueberry compote:
(makes about 2 cups)
3 cups (350 g) fresh or frozen blueberries
2 teaspoons fresh lemon juice
2 tablespoons granulated sugar
2 tablespoons of water
A tiny pinch of salt

To make the blueberry compote: combine all the compote ingredients in a small saucepan. Place over medium-low heat and bring to a simmer. Cover with a lid slightly ajar and simmer, stirring occasionally, for 10 to 12 minutes, until the blueberries are soft, swimming in their juice, and jammy.

The compote keeps in an airtight container in the refrigerator for 2 weeks.

OATMEAL AND BANANA PANCAKES

These fluffy, delicious, and nutritious pancakes are my go-tos. You can add in anything you like, such as blueberries or chocolate chips, or simply make them as is and top with butter and maple syrup. Leftover pancakes are great cold with almond butter.

Serves 4

½ cup (120 ml) almond, oat, or coconut milk beverage
2 eggs
1 banana, broken into pieces
1½ cups (135 g) oat flour
2 teaspoons baking powder
½ teaspoon salt
1 teaspoon vanilla extract
Butter

In a blender, combine the almond milk, eggs, banana, flour, baking powder, salt, and vanilla and blend until smooth.

In a large skillet, melt 1 tablespoon butter over medium-high heat until it starts to sizzle. Ladle the batter onto skillet making pancakes in any size you like. Flip when bubbles start to form, 2 to 3 minutes per side. Serve with butter and maple syrup.

MUHAMMARA TOAST WITH SOFT-BOILED EGG, ARUGULA, AND SESAME SEEDS

We figured every café has to have a toast, and this is the one we serve at ours. We spread it thickly with rich, flavorful *muhammara* and top it with a soft-boiled egg, peppery arugula, and toasted sesame seeds for a very special brunch item.

Serves 2

2 eggs
Extra virgin olive oil
2 pieces sourdough bread, sliced 1 inch thick
Muhammara-Inspired Red Pepper and Walnut Dip (page 24)
2 handfuls arugula
Squeeze of fresh lemon juice
Sprinkle of toasted sesame seeds (see page 9)
Salt and freshly ground black pepper

To soft boil the eggs, bring a small saucepan filled with water to a boil over high heat. Reduce the heat to medium and place the eggs in the water. Bring back to a slow boil and cook for 6 minutes. Remove from the heat and place in a bowl filled with cold water.

Meanwhile, drizzle some olive oil into a large skillet set over medium heat. Add the sourdough slices and toast until crispy, about 2 minutes per side.

To assemble the toast, spread each piece of toast thickly with the *muhammara*. Peel the eggs, place a whole egg on each piece of toast, and sprinkle with a little salt.

In a small bowl, toss the arugula with a little olive oil, a squeeze of lemon juice, and a sprinkle of salt. Place a handful of arugula on top of each toast and sprinkle with sesame seeds and some freshly ground black pepper.

SPANAKOPITA STRIFTI (TWISTY SPINACH PIE)

One of my favorite places to shop is Titan Foods in Astoria, Queens. It is a Greek grocery shop, the only one of its kind in New York City. It has its own bakery with an impressive array of displayed baked goods that makes you feel like you're right in the center of Athens, and the grumpy manager really seals the deal.

When we make the pilgrimage to Titan in the morning, we often get a frappe and a crispy spiral spinach pie that hits the spot. This is my homemade version, which is a little lighter. It's fun to pull apart and eat in crispy pieces.

Makes 6 coiled pies

1 bunch scallions, white and light green parts chopped
1 pound (450 g) fresh spinach, chopped
½ cup (10 g) fresh dill, chopped
1 cup (150 g) crumbled Greek or French feta
1 egg, lightly beaten

1 (1-pound / 454-g) package phyllo dough, thawed
Extra virgin olive oil
Salt and freshly ground black pepper

Preheat the oven to 375°F (190°C) and line two baking sheets with parchment paper.

Add a drizzle of olive oil, the scallions, and a pinch of salt to a medium skillet. Place over medium heat and cook until softened, about 3 minutes, then add the spinach. Cook until the spinach is wilted, about another 3 minutes, then add the dill. Stir to incorporate and cook for another minute. Remove from the heat and place the mixture in a sieve or drainer set over a bowl. Allow the mixture to cool and gently press with the back of a spoon to remove excess liquid from the spinach mixture.

Place the drained spinach in a bowl and add the crumbled feta and freshly ground black pepper. At this point—before adding the egg—taste the mixture and adjust the seasoning. Whisk in the egg and set aside.

Pour about ½ cup (120 ml) olive oil into a bowl. Prepare your phyllo by laying it out and covering it with a moist towel so it doesn't dry out.

Place one phyllo sheet in front of you oriented horizontally and brush with olive oil using a pastry brush. Repeat and layer with 3 additional sheets of phyllo. Add 2 tablespoons of the filling and spread it into a tube shape just inside the bottom edge. Gently roll it up so you have a long tube filled with the spinach mixture. Gently roll into a spiral, brush with more olive oil, and place on a baking sheet. Repeat until all the filling is used.

Bake until golden brown and crispy, 35 to 40 minutes. Serve warm or at room temperature.

KOULOURAKIA ME TAHINI (TAHINI BISCUITS WITH ORANGE AND CINNAMON)

This is one of the most revered recipes my yiayia taught me. *Koulourakia* are a barely sweetened biscuit, usually in a circle, or *koulouri*, shape and eaten dipped into a Greek coffee or as a quick snack. *Koulourakia* ingredients vary to reflect the seasons in Greece. Sometimes they are made with grape must (grape syrup), sometimes wine, tahini, or butter. My favorite version is this one, made with orange, tahini, and olive oil then covered in sesame seeds. This is a recipe for Lenten *koulourakia* usually eaten during the forty-day fasting period before Easter when no dairy or meat is allowed. They are barely sweet and have an addictive, perfectly crumbly texture. They always remind me of summertime in Aegina, the kitchen covered in flour and scented with tahini, orange, and cinnamon.

Makes about 3 dozen cookies

½ cup (120 ml) extra virgin olive oil
½ cup (120 ml) tahini
1 cup (240 ml) fresh orange juice
1 cup (200 g) granulated sugar
4 cups (480 g) all-purpose flour, plus more if needed
1 teaspoon baking powder

1 teaspoon baking soda
4 teaspoons ground cinnamon
2 teaspoons kosher salt
1 tablespoon honey
½ cup (120 ml) water
¼ cup (40 g) sesame seeds

Preheat the oven to 350°F (180°C). Line two baking sheets with parchment paper.

In a large bowl, whisk together the olive oil, tahini, orange juice, and sugar. In a separate bowl, whisk together the flour, baking powder, baking soda, cinnamon, and salt. Slowly add the flour mixture to the wet ingredients and knead together until you have a smooth, soft dough. If the dough feels sticky, add another spoonful of flour and briefly knead again. Let the dough rest for about 20 minutes. Working with a heaping tablespoon of dough at a time, roll out into a 7-inch rope as thick as your thumb (about

½-inch). Press the two ends together to form a 3-inch circle and place on the prepared baking sheet. Repeat with the remaining dough.

Whisk the honey into the water in a small bowl. Using your finger or a pastry brush, wet the top of the *koulouraki*, then gently press into the sesame seeds.

Bake for 13 to 15 minutes, until golden brown on the bottoms and lightly toasted on top. Allow to cool and serve at room temperature. They will keep for up to 2 weeks in an airtight container.

THANK YOU

To my dad, who tirelessly read and edited this book over and over again. I could not have done this without you and without all those ice cream trips. Thank you from the bottom of my heart. To my mom, who created and shares these memories with me, thank you—I love you both.

Urs Fischer, it's always an honor to work with you. To have your artwork, brilliance, humor, and sensitivity grace the pages of this book is inspiring. Thanks for always pushing me to do my very best.

Cassandra MacLeod, your photographs and anything you touch are beautiful and thoughtful. Thank you for taking this project on with me during such a crazy time, running up and down a garden, and getting that sticky date cake shot.

Domie Clausen, you've done it again—you're a typography genius! Your design work is impeccable, thoughtful, and beautiful. We might just move in next door to you in Milan for endless espressos and prosciutto.

Natasha Price, thank you for understanding just how much lemon and olive oil goes into every one of these dishes and for your patient recipe testing. You even answered all of my emails and texts (and there were so many).

Jaz Harold, you are, as always, the very best at what you do and thanks for sticking with me and dealing with all those images.

Chad Moore, you are the fastest photographer I have ever met. Thanks for your awesome photographs and surprising me with Annie, the best photo assistant in town.

Kari Stuart, can you believe it's done? Thank you for reading a million of my book proposals, believing in me so fully, and being an integral part of this entire process. You are agent extraordinaire.

Julie Will, the superstar editor of this book, you understood right from the start what it is about. I'm forever awed by the breadth of your ability. Pens down!

The whole team at Harper Wave, thanks for bringing me into your fold. You guys are a cool crew, and I am now a Microsoft Word expert thanks to you. (Emma!)

Miriam Stone, so many phone calls, so much support, thank you.

John B., your kindness, support, and listening skills made so much more possible. Thank you.

Aly Mostel, you are a star. Thank you for all your help, always.

To the people who helped bring this book to life each in their own way: Abby Haywood, Jo Sander, Angela Kunicky, Annie Roth, Leia Ignacio, Laurie Ellen Pellicano, Isobel Herbold, Palmer Thompson-Moss, Nicholas Newcomb, Hellenius Botanicals, Ioanna Pantazopoulou, Katerina Chelioti, Margarita Inez Papakosta, Robin and Elena Eagleton, Julia Eagleton, Charles Inglis, Flora Hanitijo, John Carson, Julia Sherman, Adam Katz, Shoaib Kamil, Josh Krafchin, Rachel Katwan, Julie Miller, Amy Dehuff, Randi Mates, Pali Kashi, Rich Porter, Mike McDonnough, Suzy Fauria, Luke Alvine, and Sanne Vanderveen.

The amazing PS1 crew: Thank you, Kate Fowle, Jose Ortega, Alison Cuzzolino, Molly Kurzius, Sam Denitz, Amber Sasse, Victoria Reis, and Eva Cruz. In various ways, you all have allowed and guided the making of this book. Thank you and the deepest appreciation to Agnes Gund.

To the *Mina's Café* crew, past and present, you know who you are. THANK YOU for making it all happen!

Daphne Lopez, thank you for your friendship and your support, and for talking about roasting vegetables with me in great detail. I'll see you in the rainbows.

To my family, aka the people I cannot live without: Alex Eagleton—you stepped in and did everything possible to give me the time to get this book done and so much more. I love you, you're my favorite, thank you forever! Sophia Eagleton, you're an inspiration. Thank you for being you and also for your playlists. Apollo Eagleton, my little whippersnapper of a boy, thank you for the endless cuddles and granola-making skills. I love the three of you more than words will ever express. Thank you for being my people.

INDEX

(Page references in *italics* refer to illustrations.)

ABOUT THE AUTHOR

MINA STONE is the author of *Cooking for Artists* and a career chef. For years she cooked delicious lunches at Urs Fischer's Brooklyn-based art studio as well as gallery dinners for New York's art world. In 2019 she opened her own restaurant, *Mina's*, housed within MoMA's PS1 in Long Island City, Queens.

w/ onions in

Desserts

✓ portokalopita + blackberries

cinnamon + walnut shortbreads
Macerated blueberries

coconut balls ☆

Ice cream cake ☆
Strawberries + cinnamon
mascarpone ☆

banofee pie ☆

date cake w/
tahini toffee ☆

coconut clove cake w/ blood oranges

as end)
→ much ?

2 hu
salted
olive oil
lemon
salt

mug water
gre

carrot

cucum

craek

dat

MUSAKA!
Roasted Brocolli
Persian noodle soup
soup, yogurt
sesame seeds

drop into
food goods

R

li

cr